JOHN SAINSBURY'S
ROUTER WORKSHOP

JOHN SAINSBURY'S
ROUTER WORKSHOP

David & Charles

A CIP catalogue record for this book
is available from the British Library

ISBN 0 7153 9162 3 (Hardback)
ISBN 0 7153 0219 1 (Paperback)

First published 1988
Reprinted 1990, 1991, 1993, 1995
First published in paperback 1994
Reprinted 1995

Typeset by ABM Typographics Ltd, Hull,
and printed in Great Britain
by Butler & Tanner Ltd, Frome, Somerset
for David & Charles
Brunel House   Newton Abbot   Devon

Contents

Introduction

The router must be regarded as a modern tool and in recent times it has become a very popular one for both the craftsman and the home woodworker. Many manufacturers stock machines which suit both the pocket and the needs of the man working in his home workshop, while there are more sophisticated models which meet the extending demands of the high quality woodcraft workshop.

In spite of its multiplicity of uses, the router is an extremely uncomplicated tool, easy to set up and quite simple to use. A quick glance at the number and variety of cutters on offer immediately indicates the wide applications available to the woodworker who masters its use.

The popularity of the tool is also indicated by the number of attachments, jigs and fixtures which have been designed to increase the uses to which the tool can be put: from simple routing of grooves and rebates, through carving, to joint making and wood turning. Indeed, the tool can be attached to a wood turning lathe and also to various types of benches where it converts to a spindle moulder.

Man-made timber in its many forms can be cut with great accuracy and a splendid finish can be attained, thanks to the introduction of cutters in high-speed steel (HSS), solid tungsten-carbide (TC) and tungsten-carbide tipped (TCT). Many of these alloy router cutters can be used for working plastic laminates much used in the home, for plastics, and for most of the metals such as aluminium, copper, brass, and gilding metal.

It is hoped that this book will guide you safely through the early stages to the point where problem-solving and the execution of various pieces of craftwork can be carried out without difficulty, in complete safety, and with considerable pleasure.

1 What to Look for in a Router

A decision as to which router to buy can only be made in the light of the occupation or the interests of the buyer, and the uses to which the router is to be put. Obviously, if it is to be used in trade, due consideration will have to be given as to the type of timber, the size of the jobs to be tackled and the degree of use. The router must be adequate for the task, as the ability to be used without overloading is a prime necessity.

The serious amateur woodworker may well require the same standards as the professional craftsman, particularly bearing in mind that, as he becomes familiar with the machine, he will quickly realise that he has at his command a workshop in it-

1 Elu 177E router (plunge type)

self. On the other hand, the average DIY worker who tackles the odd job or three occasionally will not need to interest himself in the more professional style of tool.

As always, the cost must be taken into account. The frequent user will be able to assess the time-saving factor and the ease of working together with the high quality of finish, and write off the cost of the machine; while the serious craftsman may balance the cost against the versatility of the machine, and count this as sufficient argument to justify the outlay. The casual user would be well advised to consider the less expensive model which will serve his needs, while looking carefully at the competitive prices along the High Street.

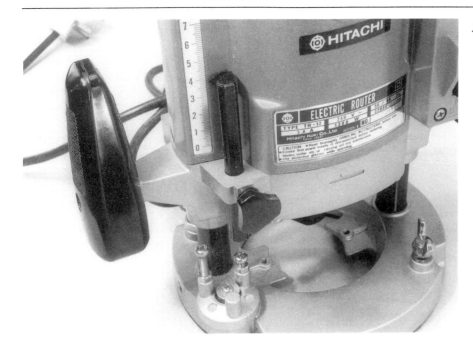

2 Hitachi rotary turret

DESIGN FEATURES AND DESIRABLE ACCESSORIES

Vast improvements have been made in router design in recent years, and much of the setting-up 'hassle' has been removed. Many old-style routers had to be depth-fed and this was handled in a number of ways, but modern routers tend to be of the plunge-type which needs only the setting of a depth gauge before commencing work to ensure accuracy and complete control. Many of the leading manufacturers are offering the plunge-type and it is my preference, having handled a fair number of the several kinds.

Our terms of reference for a satisfactory router can be clearly stated as follows:

a It should be a plunge-type as shown in the photograph.

b It should have a combination fence which will make possible both straight and curved cutting.

c It should be fitted with a depth gauge, preferably in combination with a pre-set rotary turret, which makes for fast settings in repetitive work.

d The handles should be designed to fit the hand, and positioned close to the base so that the operator has perfect control; as in Fig 2.

e It should have a collet chuck with spanner adjust-ment providing security for the cutter and safety for the user. In the case of machines with 12.7mm (½in) capacity, smaller sizes of collets should be available in both imperial and metric dimensions.

f The style of base is important, with square edges on at least two opposite sides. This enables the router to be used without a fence but with a strip of timber tacked or cramped on to the work to serve as a guide.

g A fully protected safety switch should be close at hand to enable the power to be cut off speedily, and it should be positioned in such a way that the power cannot be accidentally switched on.

h Suitably weighted springing is necessary to allow the base to retract, but it should not be so heavy as to make plunging difficult.

i Suitable locking screws, fitted with springs and washers should be provided to prevent slackening when the router is running. Adequate locking is also needed for the depth bar.

j Depth indication should be in both metric and imperial measures to meet the requirements of old and young users and, of course, markets in other countries. The markings should be clearly visible – the markings engraved on some routers are far from satisfactory and often inaccurate. This is possibly better than some instances where the accuracy is good but the security of the metal strip (which is often glued in place) is doubtful. Some routers have no markings, which may be an advantage, as the user has to set his measure from a rule or make a setting device for himself. A useful addition (seen on one machine) is a magnifier which moves along with the setting.

k   The handle (or knob) which doubles as a depth-setting retaining device on some models should be adequate to the task, and not require excessive movement either to the right or left to ensure locking and unlocking. Withdrawal of the cutter from the work should be instant and positive, and the spring-lever type positioned close to one of the handles is much more satisfactory, as it can be operated with the finger or thumb.

which an extraction hose can be fitted is very desirable.

o   A fitted guard can sometimes get in the way or obscure visibility. The design should be such as to allow the cuttings to get away and at the same time prevent the entry of the fingers – an almost impossible task!

p   Unfortunately, few makers pay the attention they should to the material used in the making of the base. This should be transparent and, at the same time, scratchproof. I have tried making them from Perspex but they require constant attention and polishing to keep them free from scratches. The lower edges of any base should be radiused, making it easy to move the router; as in Fig 4.

3 Plunge locking on the Hitachi

4 Elu 177E base with forward edge radiused

l   There should be a good field of vision around the cutter to enable the user to check the accuracy of the cutter during working.

m   While the addition of a safety guard and an extraction nozzle sometimes tends to obscure visibility, the former must be present at all times, if available and, if the operator is to see the cutter in operation at all, then a satisfactory method of dust and chip control extraction is a 'must'.

n   The machine should be so designed as to ensure a good down draught from the motor which will blow the waste dust and chips away from the point of cut. The addition of an attachment to

q   The motor itself should be protected against the ingress of dust and chips by being fitted with gauze or a perforated panel at the air intake point on the body.

r   A flat top allows the router to be inverted on the bench for ease of access to the collet: see Fig 5.

s   Routers for general use should have at least 24,000 rpm and 600 watts input, and the depth of plunge should be 51mm (2in) or greater.

t   Care must also be taken when choosing the size of the collet. It's disastrous to find only metric-size cutters available when you have a collet which only accepts imperial.

5 Elu 177E inverted to illustrate flat top

u Availability of spares is vital, although most routers are extremely reliable.
v Check also that the supplier has arrangements for servicing.
w Some additional accessories which ought to be easily available are: a fine depth adjusting bar; guide bushes; a fine fence adjusting device; a circular cutting attachment; a follower for copying, and a trimmer guide.

Although these are not essential, they will greatly increase the versatility of the machine.

SPECIAL FEATURES OF HEAVY-DUTY INDUSTRIAL ROUTERS

a Horsepower must always be adequate to the task and models are available from the average ⅞ hp up to 2 hp.
b The design of the handles must also suit the heavier tasks given to the machine. Some are fitted with one D-shaped handle and a single knob, while others have two D-type handles; one machine has a single handle with a built-in switch and a single knob for the left hand, rather like a bench plane.
c The switches and other electrical equipment must also meet the task of cutting not only wood but also plastics, non-ferrous metals, laminates and other man-made materials.
d Provision for speeds from 8,000 to 20,000 rpm will be needed by means of electronic switches or a selection of pre-determined speeds. Some routers are fitted with a 'soft start' device which gives up to 70% less reaction torque at start-up. This ensures much longer life for the bearings, the motor and the switching. Some motors are also monitored and tested at up to 30 times per second to ensure correct cutting speeds regardless of load, and this makes for longer life for the motor and the cutters.
e Bearings in industrial routers should be of the sealed type. They should also have a fairly low decibel reading, a feature which is rarely adequately covered.
f Industrial routers should be fitted with bases built of hard and transparent material which should remain smooth over a long period. Some manufacturers have recognised the need and are fitting bases with a special coating.
g All routers should have protective insulation avoiding the need for an earth. Electric motors carrying this protection will have a mark as shown on the specification plate. The electric motor should also be suppressed to prevent interference with radio, television and similar devices, and if these two features are not present it would be illegal to sell them.

6 Double insulation mark

While the foregoing notes may not be fully comprehensive it is hoped that they will guide the potential user through intricacies of routers and their accessories, helping mistakes to be avoided. It may also help craftsmen to check the equipment they already own to ensure that it conforms to present-day standards, and to learn if there are any new accessories that could be of benefit.

2 The Router Workshop

The versatility of the router prompts me to make suggestions for the ideal router workshop. Here, I have to make decisions about the selection of equipment by mentioning brand or proprietary names – this does not in any way imply that I find others inferior or unsuitable.

The professional woodworker will obviously need a heavier and more highly powered router and correspondingly tougher equipment all round, and separate recommendations are therefore made for both the craftsman with his living to earn and the serious amateur woodworker.

THE PROFESSIONAL WOODWORKER'S WORKSHOP

Most craftsmen working in wood have tended in the last twenty years or so to add a number of portable power tools to their workaday kit, since such tools can be used on the job or in the workshop or at home. Usually the tools include a circular saw, a jig saw and, possibly, a planer; to which has now been added the router. I have borne these points in mind when selecting my kit.

TRITON work centre

Of the many work benches I have looked at and used, the Triton Mk 3 is the one I recommend, because of its many clever features. The circular saw, the jig saw and the router can all be used in conjunction with it. These machines can be inverted by a clever system of sliding tables which can be traversed across the work or held in the fixed position with the material moved across, or into, the cutter; the bench is well guarded in every mode and heavily built in sheet steel. The tolerances are close and the accuracy of cutting is probably unequalled in a workbench of this type.

We shall need the Triton bench with the addition of the router and jig saw table. While this can be set up on the normal benchtop, it is recommended that

7 *Triton Workcentre, with router and spindle moulder ready for action*

the optional folding stand should be added, and for the man who wants to move the assembly around an investment in a pair of stand wheels will speed up the work and prevent injuries to his back.

A heavy-duty router must have priority and for this bench the Hitachi TR12 model (Fig 10) will serve admirably. It's a plunge action job with a three-stage turret depth-setting for repetition work. Rated at 1,300 watts, it offers 22,000 'no-load' rpm. The collet has 12.7mm (½in) capacity and standard equipment includes two chuck sleeves to give options in cutter shank sizes. Also included is a bar holder, a template guide, a trimmer guide and the usual spanners. With a weight of 5 kg (approx 11 lb), it's the router for hard work under any conditions.

I have expressed the opinion elsewhere that dust and chip extraction is of paramount importance, particularly bearing in mind the many and varied timbers which are in use and the dangers of dust which

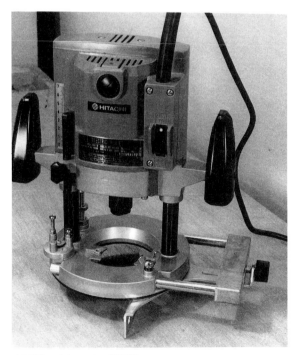

9 Triton fitted with rollers for easy movement in the workshop or on site

10 Hitachi router TR12

11 Trend staircase jig

can cause allergies and possibly be explosive. The reader would be advised to consider such equipment from the start and buy it so that it can be fitted to the installation he has chosen.

A selection of cutters can only be made with knowledge of the work programme to be undertaken, and the best advice here is – only buy when needed. Buy HSS (high-speed steel) for normal work in wood and TCT (tungsten carbide tipped) for tough grained stuff. It is advisable not to use HSS on particle board and other man-made materials such as MDF boards or plywood; always employ TCT cutters. Refer to Chapter 11 before selecting.

Any number and types of jigs can be made as the need arises for different jobs, but for staircase work the Trend staircase jig deserves consideration.

Particularly useful in making drawers and box-like kitchen furniture, the Leigh dovetailing jig, in spite of its cost, is the best of its kind since it is not only fully adjustable for size, but it can be used for through and lap dovetails in any combination of size of pin and socket. It can also be utilised for finger jointing and shortly there will appear a number of additions

which will make this jig one of the most versatile anywhere. See page 87 and Fig 156 for greater detail of the jig in use.

For extreme accuracy of depth-setting a fine adjuster is a great help but it is not essential.

A range of guide bushes is essential to avoid problems when working with templates. See page 96 for details.

A beam trammel is frequently offered as an optional extra, and where curved work within the boundaries of a circle are needed, it is a worthwhile accessory.

These, then, are my recommendations for a professional craftsman's workshop.

Elu routers and accessories

Cost will always have a bearing on the equipment we buy, but we must never lose sight of the need for versatility and lasting service. For the man who is fully conscious of his requirements and who, at the same time, wants to keep to just one or two branded names then Black & Decker Elu is undoubtedly the answer. I recommend the Elu 551 router table. It is an extremely sturdy free-standing work table which can be fitted up to incorporate a circular saw com-

12 Electronic speed setting on the Elu 177E

plete with all the refinements of the normal table saw. The router kit is complete with guards and other accessories, and also has a circuit breaker which can be conveniently attached to one of the legs of the table.

Any router of the Elu range can be fitted to this table, and here I recommend the MOF 177. I have been privileged to use the E version, and the choice of speeds has probably spoiled me for all other routers. It has a motor with 1,850 watts input and 1,100 watts output. Speeds are infinitely variable between 8,000 and 20,000 rpm – a real help to the man who works in both metal and wood (a 'must' indeed when working on window frames). The chuck capacity is 6.35mm (1/4in) or 12.7mm (1/2in) with an M12 adaptor. It has a plunge of 65mm (2 7/16in) and a maximum cutter size of 40mm (1 9/16in).

Any number of guide bushes from the Trend range can be used. Pressure guards ensure safety, and fine fence- and depth-adjusters make for great accuracy. A number of other purpose-designed aids are also available.

The full wave electrical control ensures a perfect finish, and whatever material is being cut there will be no drop-off of power under heavy load. The soft start is a splendid feature – no longer need one tend to grab the router when starting on the work, or scare oneself with a jerk start.

The Elu dovetailer solves the problems associated with this type of joint, and makes for the easy construction of cabinets, drawers and similar work.

Safety is well catered for with the Elu since the

router can be fitted with connector spouts for coupling to a vacuum outlet. If the pocket will stand it, Elu have the most outstanding high performance vacuum extractors that I have ever seen for use for this particular job – the Eve 938. These units can be coupled to two machines.

Other accessories, as previously detailed, can be added to these suggestions. To have all the equipment from one 'brand leader' is, of course, a great help when additions or repairs become necessary.

THE HOME CRAFTSMAN WORKSHOP

Much thought is needed when tackling the job of fitting up the home craftsman workshop. The cash available, the work which is envisaged, and the amount of working space will all tend to influence the choice of equipment. Having experience of that most versatile of benches – the Workmate, I looked at Black & Decker's products and found their Power Tool Table. This not only has an optional leg system which can be added but it can also be fitted to the Workmate 2 (WM750).

13 Black & Decker Workmate 2

*14 Black & Decker
Power Tool Table, on
purpose-built stand*

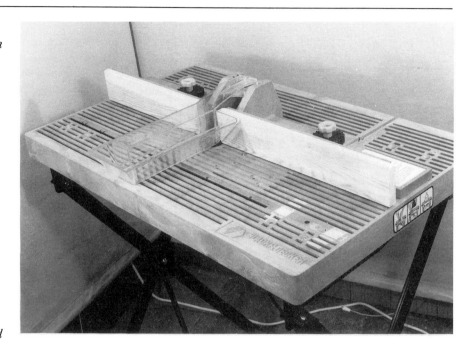

*15 Workmate with
power tool table fitted*

16 Lervad bench showing double row of dogs

A great deal of thought has been put into the design of this table and, although at first I doubted the strength of the plastic material from which it is made, I found it stood up well to the rigours of the tasks I gave it. It will hold any of the Black & Decker routers, also the Elu MOF96. The fence and guards are fine and there is provision for locking the switch.

Bearing in mind that the table will also receive both circular and jig saws, it's a splendid answer to the man with little space and not too much money in his pocket, since both the independent leg system can be folded back as it can on the Workmate 2 if this should be the choice of stand – indeed, I would much prefer the latter since it has the separate woodworking bench facility.

The workshop bench
Undoubtedly the home craftsman, particularly if he has only very little space, will have few problems with the aforementioned equipment, but for the craftsman working on his own, and the small industrial workshop, a standard workbench will be needed. The problems of holding work for routing are many, due largely to the great versatility of the machine. These cannot always be solved with the traditional English bench which has only a side vice. For many years I have used a Lervad bench which is fitted with a dog vice at the right hand end and a series of dog positions along the bench top. The reader will find this bench in many of the illustrations and take note of its versatility.

The bench with two rows of dog positions is even better, since round and uneven shapes can be held safely.

The vice (USA – vise) with a sliding bench dog incorporated into the jaw casting is fairly standard in the USA, and is usually made of metal! The Record model, originally made by Record for the North American market, could well be fitted to the traditional bench with dog positions suitably cut in the bench top. Speed is often of the essence, and the dog-vice with its special type of holding and quick release capacities must be the answer.

17 Cabinetmaker's vice with sliding dog and bench dogs

3 Safety and Parts of the Router

Any power tool can be dangerous in careless hands and none more so than the power router. Manufacturers are well aware of this and actively provide these tools with adequate notes on safety. These notes should be read carefully, indeed, it would be as well to paste them to a card and hang them up in the workshop close to the power source.

Read the booklet accompanying the router, acquaint yourself with the name of each part, and identify each one by reference to the router itself.

Learn the safety rules by heart, and follow them implicitly. Prepare the work place; don't work on a cluttered bench; and make sure that the floor space around the work bench is clear of tools, timber and the like. Shavings left around tend to polish the floor and this may make standing difficult.

Don't have other tools around, and store any parts of the router not in use in a safe place.

Make it a golden rule never to plug in the router until all adjustments have been made and a double check carried out on the security of each part. Invert the router on the bench when making adjustments. The Black & Decker 66 is automatically switched off when this is done.

Make sure that the lighting is adequate. A lamp with a flexible arm and a tungsten-filament bulb is best, since the need to see well into the point of action is often of paramount importance. Some machines have an in-built light which removes this need.

Check that the cable is undamaged, and that the plug is serviceable and correctly fused to suit the loading of the machine.

Never use the router in humid or damp situations. Working in the rain is lethal.

In order to protect against electric shock never

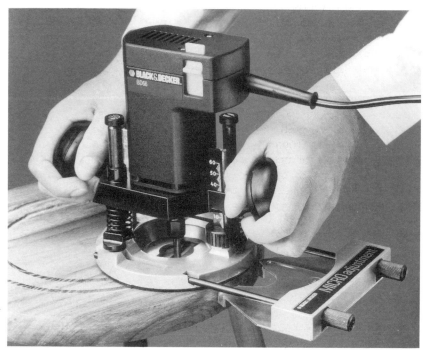

18 Black & Decker 66, with flat top and automatic switch-off when router is inverted.

19 Metal detector

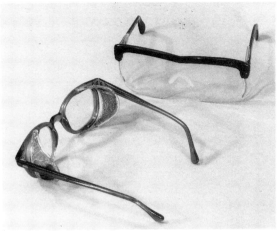

20 Protective eye shields

touch objects or pieces of furniture such as gas stoves, sinks, pipes or radiators when working with the router, since many of them are earthed.

Check that the horsepower rating of the router is adequate for the task.

Choose the cutter to suit the material and be doubly sure of its security within the chuck (the shank should be pushed well inside to be held firmly by the collet jaws). A loose cutter can fall out and fly from the machine at great speed.

Never work with the router in an area where inflammable liquids are in use or in store, since the sparks from the motor may bring about an explosion.

Don't have an audience, especially children.

Make sure that the work piece is securely held (see page 54 for suggestions). Both hands should be free to operate the router.

Check the timber for metal in the shape of nails or screws, particularly if using reclaimed materials. Striking an unseen piece of metal is not only a frightening experience but also a dangerous one. There are a number of tools which can detect hidden metal.

Always wear suitable clothing, and avoid loose clothing which may fall into or across the path of the router and spell danger for the operator; it can also obscure the view. The boiler suit or coverall would be most suitable. Even jewellery can be a hazard. Long hair needs a net or a secure cap. When working outdoors, be sure to wear non-slip shoes.

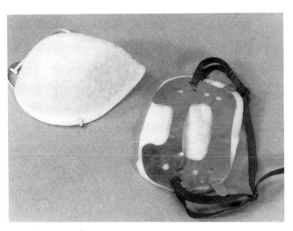

21 Dust masks

22 Ear muffs

We cannot ignore the dangers of flying chips, knots and dust, and the wise craftsman will protect his eyes with goggles; his nose and throat with a dust mask; and if the noise is excessive, ear plugs or muffs. Yes; this may be a 'hassle', but it's best to be prepared. Noise is a problem with machines of this type, but manufacturers are well aware of the need for quieter operation and improvements will come.

Safety-at-work regulations have made the attachment of guards compulsory in industry, and all users both at home and at work should make use of them.

The removal of waste always presents a problem. Some routers have a small attachment which can be fitted to link up with the domestic vacuum cleaner or one of the small portable industrial units. Alternatively, a purpose-designed unit (see below) can be used; these take up little space and are extremely effective. My Triton workbench links to a wall-mounted dust extraction system called 'The Mite'.

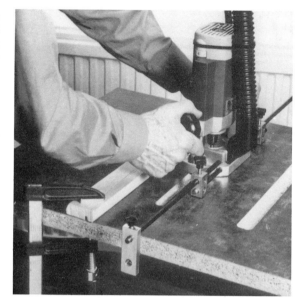

24 Elu router fitted with extraction

23 Router showing guard and waste coupling

We must pay more attention to the timbers we use, particularly in relation to the harmful effects of the dust from some of the imported ones. This is very important when routing, since one's head is very close to the cutting area and, with the cutter revolving at high speed, minute particles of dust are sent into the air. These linger long after cutting has ceased thus making extraction a matter of great importance. If the user has any doubts about the pathological effects of a particular timber he should

25 The Mite wall-mounted extraction unit

check with the timber expert or a medical authority which deals with subject (see page 131).

Never, ever, carry the machine by the cable or disconnect it by tugging the cable to pull out the plug. Always protect the cable against sharp edges, heat or destructive oils.

If the router is used attached to a table, whether inverted or in the normal mode, check that it is securely fixed. Place the guards in position, and always use a push stick to put the work through and keep the fingers well away from the cutter.

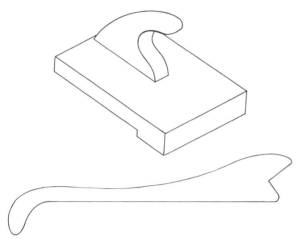

26 (a) Push block; (b) push stick

27 Push stick in use

A blunt cutter adds to the router's work load, and if the cutter is pushed too hard it may break and leave the machine at great speed, endangering the operator.

Stand firmly, avoiding an awkward and insecure stance, and check that a good stance can be retained throughout the operation. Do a dummy run before connecting up the machine.

Read the maintenance instructions carefully and follow them through.

Never change a cutter with the router plugged in.

Check the cable regularly, and should it be damaged in any way, return it to a service centre for replacement. Never join up a severed cable; this applies equally to extension cables which should be checked to ensure that they are of the correct type to take the load.

Never leave the machine plugged in for long periods.

Always make a point of cleaning the handles of the router should they become greasy or sticky.

Carry the router with the fingers well away from the switch.

Before connecting up to the mains be sure to check that the router switch is in the off position.

Hold the router firmly, and be prepared to counter the initial starting torque of the motor, although some routers are now of the 'soft start' variety which eliminates this.

Don't switch on the router with the cutter in contact with the timber. Indeed, it is good practice to start up the router free from such contact in order to check it for free rotation.

Learn to recognise the different sounds made by the router, and listen for the perfect cutting sound as opposed to a labouring one. Stop the router if a strange sound is heard and check for trouble.

Remember to feed the router in the correct direction, which is against the direction of the cutter's rotation. If a machine table is in use with the router inverted, paint an arrow on the table top to show the direction of feed: some tables are ready-marked with such an arrow.

Remember that the bit will be extremely hot immediately after use; leave it to cool before removing it or making adjustments. The carbon brushes in the electric motor may easily be replaced when worn. This is straightforward, see page 129; but be careful to use the correct brushes to suit the motor.

Check the router periodically to ensure that all safety devices are present and that all components are functioning as they should.

Check for breakages, replace parts if necessary and always with the correct spares available from the manufacturer or the service centre. Always have a faulty switch replaced at a service centre.

Proceed with caution, concentrate on the work, and if any distraction is likely to occur – stop work and switch off. Store the machine in a cupboard when not in use, away from curious little people.

If there are exposed steel parts give them a rub with a lightly oiled rag. Remember to wipe away the oil before using the router otherwise the oil will possibly mark the work.

Observe the general rules for the use of power tools. REMEMBER: SAFETY IS LARGELY IN THE HANDS OF THE USER – NEVER TAKE CHANCES

28 Elu Eve 938 Vacuum Extractor

Dust extraction

One of the most useful systems for use in small workshops as a single system, and in larger ones for coupling to a single or several machines, is the dust extraction unit called the Mite. As I have mentioned, I have one in the teaching shop. The unit is very small and can be mounted high up on a wall, as mine is, and its single filter and collection bag hangs down to just clear the floor; thus, it can be fitted into an odd corner. It is extremely quiet, which is a great advantage over many others; even a domestic vacuum cleaner makes more noise. Its pick-up ability is far superior to that of my portable industrial-type vacuum, and when coupled to the Elu 177 router it makes an excellent job, removing upwards of 80% of the waste. A complete range of coupling accessories is available.

The machine has a ¾hp motor and is fitted with a safety switch. The impeller is a heavy-duty job, perfectly balanced, and its suction is calculated as 635 cubic feet per minute (1,074m³ hour). The calico/cotton warm air filter stores 0.113m³ (4 cu ft) of waste. Total height is 1.22m (48in) which can be shortened by tying at the bottom of the bag.

Vacuum extractor

Many craftsmen having limited space will not venture into the field of large double-bag type dust extractors. In spite of its cost the real answer is the high performance vacuum extractor best seen in the Elu

Eve938. This is a well built (good looking, in fact) machine fitted with a replaceable cartridge filter which is approved for the safe handling of toxic dust. The lightweight hose connects to the standard type spout which is available for fitting to most routers. It is supplied with 10 metres of cable and automatic on-off switching of the extractor. The noise level is less than that of the majority of small power tools.

Elu provide connector spouts to fit most of their power tools.

Dust extraction sets

Whenever we work in wood, dust extraction is essential, particularly when we bear in mind the wide variety of timbers available and the harmful effects of some of them. The provision of coupling gear for dust extractors on routers has now been recognised by the leading router manufacturers. One such kit is on offer from Elu; the component parts are shown in the drawing. This kit is designed to extract something in the order of 90% of the fine dust particles (sometimes referred to as 'floating microns') and 70% of the heavier material.

To obtain reasonably efficient removal of dust we need a good suction rate at the hose extraction point on the router. Thus, we need the shortest possible hose to avoid inhibiting the air flow; each additional metre of hose length over and above the three metres supplied will reduce the air flow by 5%.

29 Kress router showing safety guard and dust extraction boss

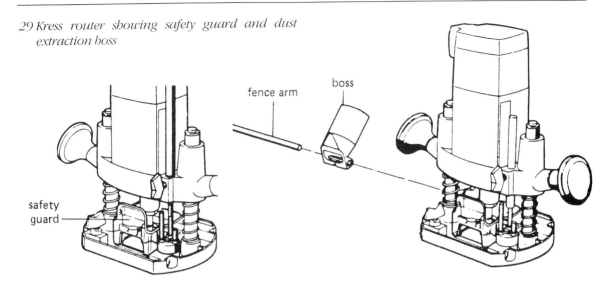

fence arm

boss

safety guard

A light routing operation will enable more dust to be removed than a heavy one. Particle board dust will be removed much more easily than softwood chips. Varying shapes in router cutters will also affect the way in which the cuttings leave the cutting point; this may well affect the pick-up. Follow the maker's instructions for fitting the gear; don't take short cuts.

Remember that when carrying out edging work much of the heavy waste will fall to the floor, but the 'micron' element will be picked up. Always empty the bag at frequent intervals and clean the filters if they are fitted.

Use an extraction unit with at least 2.12m³ (75 cfm – cubic feet per minute) extraction rate. Most domestic vacuum cleaners are capable of this – as also are the small drum type industrial vacuum cleaners.

Be careful not to distort the hose or the couplings as this will stop the free flow of air. Don't connect a secondary hose since air flow will be inhibited. Remember – minimum hose length gives maximum suction power.

Dust extraction boss

The Kress router has a dust extraction boss which is held in position by one of the fence arms. Some other routers have similar gear.

Another router has a plastic hood and hose socket.

Flexible drive

A flexible arm can be attached to a number of routers, and it is essential to secure the router to the bench top before beginning to use this type of attachment. Kress have a small clamp which slides into place in one of the fence arm holes.

Holding the router cable

Keeping the router cable out of the path of the router is often extremely difficult, especially when moving the router through quick curves as the cable tends to wrap around it.

30 Cable holder

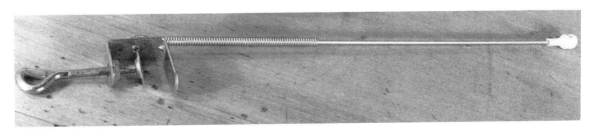

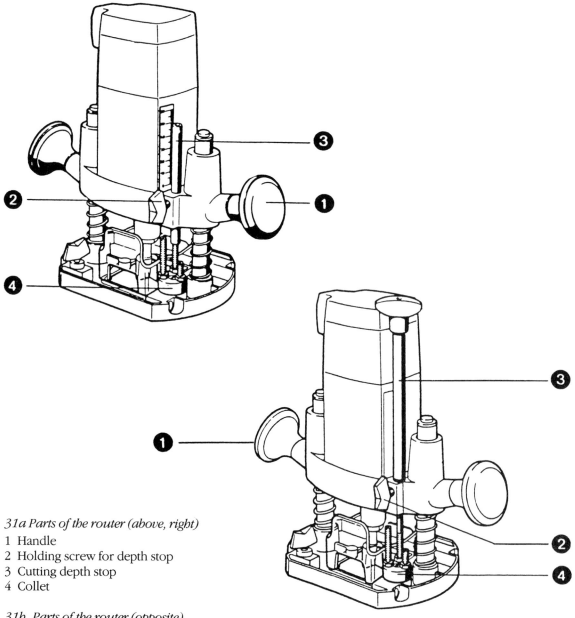

31a Parts of the router (above, right)
1 Handle
2 Holding screw for depth stop
3 Cutting depth stop
4 Collet

31b Parts of the router (opposite)

1 Cut-in and cut-out switch
2 Cord with anti-buckling sleeve
3 Motor carrier
4 Handle
5 Holding knob for securing depth setting
6 Holding screw for depth stop
7 Cutting depth stop
8 Collet

9 Base plate with guide columns
10 Turret depth stop
11 Parallel stop with interchangeable plug-type
    skids
12 Guide rods
13 Guard
14 Electronic adjusting dial
15 Flexible drive

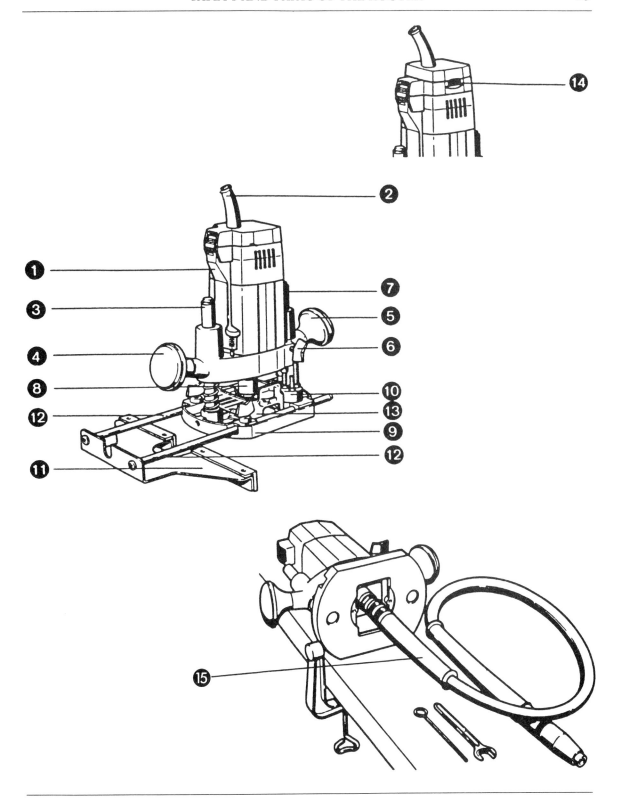

I have found an excellent solution to this problem in the shape of an attachment from my wife's ironing board. I borrowed it some time back – the wife was not pleased! It consists of a small clamp to which is attached a sprung arm; a plastic clip at the other end serves to hold the router cable. I screw the arm to a beam above the bench which keeps the cable well away from the action and it's really first rate – I'll need to buy another to keep the peace!

Horsepower

To assess the horsepower required needs some knowledge of the uses to which the router is to be put and the types of material and the sizes of cutters likely to be used. The volume of work it has to undertake, and whether it is to be in continuous use over short or long periods should also be considered.

For the casual home user a light router will serve adequately, and if the router appears to labour when used with some cutters, making two depths of cut with two passes will ensure no overload. Great care is needed when changing depth settings like this to ensure accuracy.

All routers will have a quoted rpm but it must be appreciated that this figure is without load and running free. Should the motor slow down appreciably then there is every chance that the quality of the cut will be lowered – and, indeed, the life of the router cutter itself or at least the life of its cutting edge will be shortened. Perhaps it would be wise to say – buy as much horsepower as you can afford, but not less than one horsepower. As you go up in power so the machine quality itself is improved and the cost will, of course, be greater. In making a choice look also at the specification for each router and if it doesn't have ball bearings, don't buy it. There is a new range of routers now on offer (and mentioned elsewhere in this book) which have electronic control of power, where the motor itself makes the allowance needed when certain cuts are tending to overtax it.

Router handles

Many tools suffer from inadequate hand-holding devices, and this applies to even a modern tool like the router. Most have knobs, some of which are just not big enough to give adequate grip, while others too much of a handful.

Again, we must look at the type of work which the machine has to do. Holding-down must take a certain priority, but where some real 'push' is needed the D-type handle must be preferred. These are fitted one each side of the body, or with a knob at the front and a D handle at the rear, rather like a plane. Certain it is that the latter two types offer less hand fatigue than the knob style.

The position of the handles is also important. Those routers where the handles are placed high on the body are not as steady in handling as those on which the handles are positioned closer to the work.

Depth adjustment

Four methods are in use:
a. The most popular is the plunging-type. These are spring-loaded, allowing the router cutter to be retracted above the base of the router. When action is required the router is pushed downwards, stopping at a depth which is pre-set. This is perhaps the easiest and safest approach to routing.
b. Rack and pinion. In this design the cutter depth is set by turning a screw to actuate the pinion which works in a rack. The router has to be lowered on to the work, which takes a little bit of practice. I have had one of these fitted to a router table which was made twenty years ago – its great advantage is the positive setting of the depth of cut with no possibility of the motor slipping.
c. Spiral setting. In this type the body rotates through a spiral to set the depth, and once again the machine must be lowered on to the work. The spiral is locked – usually with a thumb-type screw.
d. Ring adjustment. Here the setting is carried out by turning a body ring; once again, the setting is locked by a turnscrew. The setting is easily checked against markings on the ring itself which correspond with a set-mark on the body.

Switch gear

Instant cut-off is necessary with routers and often this is not quite as easy as it might be, due to the type and position of the switch itself. The switch should be so positioned that the user can have both hands holding the machine at all times. There are a number of different types; the most often seen being:

Trigger
Toggle
Rocker
Slider

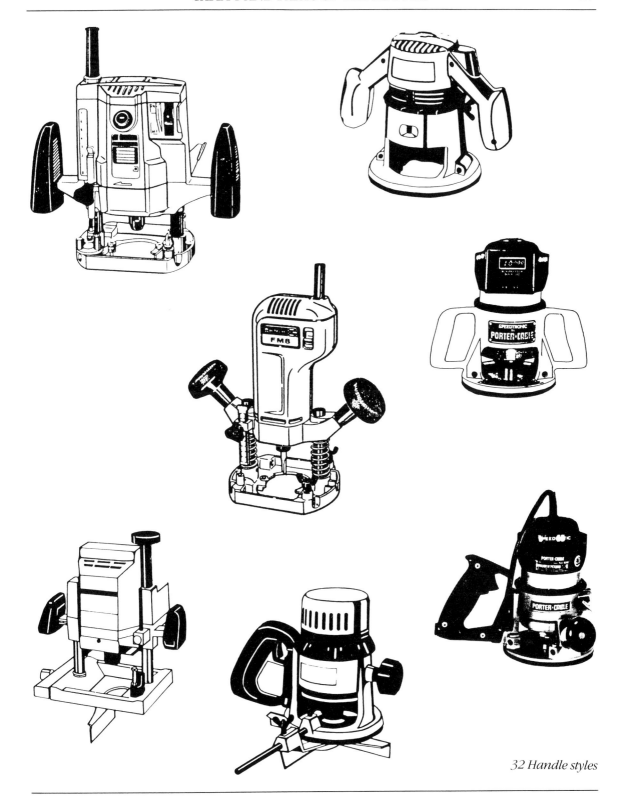

32 Handle styles

33 Trigger switch by Porter Cable

34 Toggle switch by Porter Cable

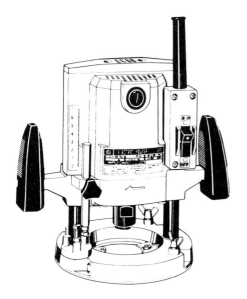

35 Rocker switch by Hitachi

36 Slider switch by Elu – under the thumb

37 Slider switch by Kress

The trigger is built in with the hand grip, and is probably the best of the four since the user is able to hold the router from the moment of starting to the point of stopping. In other words, the complete cutting process is firmly in both hands. One disadvantage is that unless the user takes great care when picking up the router, he can inadvertently start the motor at the same time. I make a practice of lifting the router with the left hand knob to avoid this, but it can be a little tricky when the machine is set up in the table position.

Sliders work well and are quite positive in their action, but often, because of the positioning of the switch on the body of the router, it becomes quite impossible to actuate the switch without taking one hand away from a handle. This type of switch is best seen in the Kress router where the switch is a long slider with finger/thumb positions at both ends, giving instant control of electrical action at all times.

Rocker switches are quite positive, but, once again, their positions are vital. They happen to be a pet hate of mine since one of my early machines had a rocker switch which was most difficult to find by touch.

Toggle switches call for good designing to give ease of access. A great advantage with this type of switch is when the router is inverted and fitted to a table. An early Black & Decker model of mine gives instant access in this position and remote contact when used normally.

I think I should select the Kress style switch when writing a specification for the dream machine!

Chucks

The simplest method of holding the router cutter is seen in a number of cheaper machines. It consists of a straight sleeve into which the cutter slides; the cutter is held in place with a small grub screw inserted in the side. This is probably quite satisfactory for the casual user but, over a period of time, wear can take place on the grub screw threads. This makes it difficult to keep the cutter firmly in place, even when using cutters having a flat machined on one side against which the grub screw locates to prevent them loosening under load. It must be noted that very few cutters are available with the flat, though the user can of course easily grind a small flat himself.

The best method is easily the collet. This has jaws which can be tightened down using spanners, one holding the machine spindle and the other screwing down on the collet body. Most medium size routers have 6.35mm (¼in) or 6mm diameter collets, but for heavy duty work a 12.7mm (½in) or 12mm collet is needed. A number of the bigger machines have several options, made possible by using sleeves and additional collets. Only the user can make a decision here, depending on the type of work and the work load.

4 Selecting a Router

A look at some of the currently available routers will give the reader a chance to make a short list of routers which may meet his needs. It would be most unwise to select from a catalogue; any tool of this kind should be handled in a store before purchase, and a chat with a knowledgeable assistant may be well-advised.

HEAVY-DUTY ROUTERS

For the professional craftsman a close examination of those routers for heavy duty will provide an interesting experience. Hitachi Koki Co of Japan list two machines which fit into this category. The TR8 plunging type router is a double-insulated heavy-duty job which carries the 'double square' safety mark. It features a three stage turret and is fitted with a 6.35mm (¼in) capacity collet chuck. Power rating is 730 watts with a speed of 24,000 rpm. The router comes complete with a straight fence fitted with two fence bars, a bar holder, a guide bush and two spanners. It's heavily built with the handles canted to place the hands in excellent control of the machine. A large locking lever serves to hold the depth of plunge, a much more positive action than twisting one of the holding knobs which is the method used in most of the smaller routers. The router is well ventilated and handles heavy cuts without problems.

The TR12 is an almost identical router but is much heavier – 5.0 kg (approx. 11 lb) against 2.9 kg (approx 6½ lb) of the TR8. Rated at 1200 watts, the chuck has a 12.7mm (½in), capacity, but the machine comes complete with two chuck sleeves, which allow smaller shank cutters to be used. Revolutions at 22,000 per minute are ideal for this type of machine. See Fig 10 page 13.

The Porter Cable Company of Jackson, Tennessee, are no longer in association with Rockwell and have a number of extremely fine routers. The model 690 is rated at 8 amp with a speed of 22,000 rpm. Its

39 Porter Cable Router No. 691

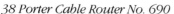

38 Porter Cable Router No. 690

40 Porter Cable Router No. 518

chuck capacity is 12.7mm (½in) but 6.35mm (¼in) and 9.52mm (⅜in) cutters can be fitted. It has a threaded motor housing and a micrometer setting ring, clearly marked for accurate sighting. Weighing in at 3.96 kg (8¾ lb), the 1½hp motor gives high torque power. The base is replaceable and the body flat-topped to make for fast, easy cutter changes.

Model 691 is similar in capacities to the 690, but is fitted with a trigger-type switch located in a D-handle.

Model 518 is the pride of the range. Here we have a 5-speed 3hp production router capable of tackling any job. It has maximum torque at five selectable speeds from 10,000 to 22,000 rpm; thus speeds can be set exactly to suit the material. The motor is monitored at 30 times per second to maintain desired cutting speed regardless of the load; this ensures longer motor life and adds to the life of the cutters. It has a 'soft start' which provides between 50% to 70% less reaction to torque at start-up. Less in-rush surges of current make for less tripping of circuit breakers. It is, apparently, 10 decibels quieter than most routers at lower speeds. It is also fitted with a heavy duty external cord strain-relief protector. The machine is a really neat looking job, fitted with two D-type handles low down and there is micrometer depth setting and a replaceable base. It has 15 amp rating, a 12.7mm (½in) chuck with 6.35mm (¼in) optional chuck. Weighing in at 8.50 kg (18¾ lb), this must be the 'Rolls Royce of Routers'.

It must be remembered that most American machines are rated at 110 volts to conform with OSHA safety regulations in the USA. Readers in other countries should check before purchase.

Bosch, the West German company, have a number of professional routers, one of the heaviest being the 1603. It has a power input of 1150 watts and a no-load speed of 25,500 rpm. With a horsepower of 1¾, it weighs 5.67 kg (12½ lb). Fitted with low-set knobs, it has the usual fittings supplied as standard. Two lower rated power input routers have 6.35mm (¼in) collets.

Makita, another well known name in power tools, has several heavy-duty models. Perhaps the most important of these is the 3608B with an input of 500 watts and a no-load speed of 23,000 rpm. Its chuck capacity is 6.35mm (¼in). The router has micrometer setting, and is flat topped so that it will stand securely on the bench when inserting cutters. An

41 Bosch Router No. 1603

unusual feature is that the knobs are set on arms which slope off the top of the machine body.

The 3601B is rated at 930 watts, and 23,000 rpm no-load speed. Its D-handle has an integral switch. It weighs in at 3.5 kg (7lb 11oz).

The 3600B plunge type router has an input of 1,500 watts and runs at 22,000 rpm. It has the usual fittings, and also a fine depth control with a plunge capacity of 60mm (2⅜in). Again, we find the 12.7mm (½in) chuck capacity as standard. The machine weighs 5 kg (11 lb).

The Elu range of routers is probably the most attractive both as regards design and versatility. They seem to be constantly updating their equipment in the light of developments and the needs of the market. At the same time, they have a wide range of accessories suitable for the needs of most craftsmen.

A mid-range router is the MOF 131. This model has a no-load speed of 18,000 rpm with a motor input of 1200 watts. It weighs 5.5 kg (12lb 2oz) and is available in both 115 and 220 voltages. The collet accepts a 12.7mm (½in) shank cutter but 9.25mm (⅜in) and 6 to 12mm diameters are also available; maximum cutter size is 40mm (1⁹⁄₁₆in). The plunge stroke maximum is 65mm (2⁹⁄₁₆in). The router is fitted with a two-column guide, a turret depth-stop with three stages, and a quick-acting plunge clamp.

42 Elu Router No. 131

The router comes complete with a parallel fence, a bush holder and a 30mm (1³⁄₁₆in) template guide bush, together with the usual spanners.

Heavy-duty routers of advanced design are seen in the 177 and 177E. The 177 has a motor input of 1600 watts, an output of 960 watts, and a no-load speed of 20,000 rpm from motors of either 115 or 220 voltage. The machine weighs 5.1kg (11lb 6oz) and has a standard collet set offering 6.35mm (¼in), 12.7mm (½in) diameters, and m12 x 1 adaptor which is a threaded insert used for holding cutters tapped with the same thread. 6mm, 8mm, 10mm, 12mm and 9.25mm (³⁄₈in) collets are also available, and 40mm (1⁹⁄₁₆in) diameter cutters are the maximum accepted. The three positional turret stop adjustment allows excellent reading of depth being fitted with a scale magnifier. At the same time, rack and pinion depth-stop adjustment makes for greater accuracy and consistency.

The base, which is plastic-coated for easy running, has straight and curved edges to allow for accurate guidance against battens and curved templates. A plunger switch which is located in the handle provides greater safety because a firm grip can be maintained on the machine when switching off. A fine

router which looks as good as it is.

The 177E, which I have used extensively, Fig 1 p8 has all the features of the 177 but its motor is more powerful, having an input of 1850 watts and an output of 1100 watts, with infinitely variable speeds between 8,000 and 20,000 rpm. Here we see the full-wave electronic control for the first time from Elu. This ensures that the same clean, accurate finish is achieved in all kinds of timber, aluminium, and plastic, since the automatic speed control prevents any serious decrease of speed under load. Optimum speed can be selected to suit the cutter diameter for better all round performance, the rule being that the larger the cutter diameter, the slower the speed should be. Here we have the easy start, which means no off-putting jerk when the motor is switched on – which must be a considerable bonus with a router of this power. Another great advantage with slower speeds is that possible scorching of the timber is reduced when working freehand. The router has all the other advanced features seen in the 177.

Ryobi produce a number of excellent heavy-duty machines. The R500 is suitable for production use, having an input of 1500 watts, rated horsepower of 2, and a no-load speed of 22,000 rpm. It will plunge to 60mm (2³⁄₈in) and its depth stop, working off a turret, is operated by the thumb. While its collet capacity is stated at 12mm (½in), it is equipped with a collet adaptor which accepts various sizes of cutters (this feature is an excellent one also seen in a number of other machines). The design is such that there is excellent visibility around the cutter.

There are two other models with a rating of 2 horsepower. They are the R220 with an input wattage of 1,000 and no-load speed of 23,000 rpm; and the R330 with an input of 1400 watts, and a no-load speed of 24,000 rpm. They both have the 12mm (½in) capacity with a main body stroke of 20mm (³⁄₄in); the depth setting is through a body spiral. All the usual attachments are available, and the plastic sole plate on the base is noted as non-marring to protect the work surface from scratches. The R331 is a newer addition to the range but, in this case, is fitted with a D-type handle and a knob – all other features are similar to the R330.

There are a number of companies manufacturing medium-duty routers which are suitable for professionals carrying out lighter tasks as well as for the serious home craftsman.

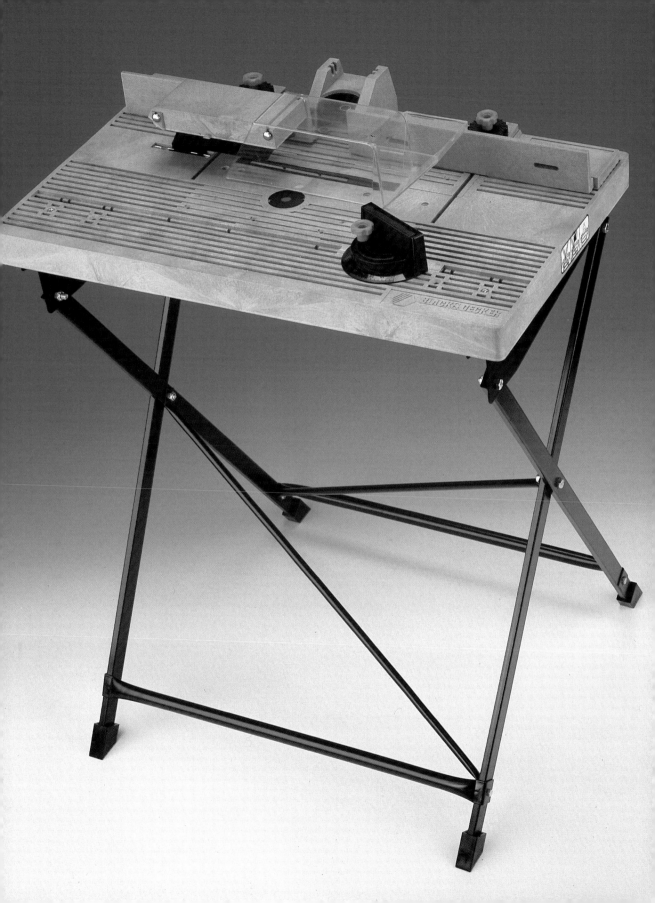

44 Hitachi FM8

43 Kress Router No. 600

A fine example, having electronic switching which allows a selection of speeds at the turn of a button, is the Kress – made in West Germany. It has an input rating of 600 watts and no-load speeds ranging from 8,000 to 24,000 rpm. The fitted collet is of 6mm (¼in) capacity, but an Imperial ¼ is suitable as an optional extra. It is suggested that the maximum cutting diameter of any cutter should be limited to 30mm (1¹³/₁₆in), while maximum depth of cut is 46mm (1³/₁₆in). The router is fitted with a parallel fence which has precise setting adjustment and changeable slide guides. The springs of the plunge mechanism are just right for strength; on some routers they can be over-strong, making life difficult. The switch is the best yet, as it is fitted to the side of the machine in the form of a slide which is easily accessible to the fingers at all times. Such a switch is a very desirable feature, particularly in a panic situation! As the machine is fitted with a turret, depth setting is simplified and readings are easily seen on the scale adjacent to the setting bar. Optional extras available include a precision depth setting screw, a beam compass for circular work, a 24mm (¹⁵/₁₆in) guide sleeve, and a flexible shaft.

Hitachi have the FM8 in this range. This is produced in a number of different voltages with an input of 640 watts and a no-load speed of 27,000 rpm.

45 Hitachi FM8 with motor removed

Of the plunging variety, its capacity is 51mm (2in). Collet size is 6.35mm (¼in) with optional chuck sleeves of 8mm x 6mm and 8mm x 6.35mm sleeves – giving collet sizes of 8mm and 6mm. An excellent feature is the ease with which the body can be removed from the body frame and this permits its assembly into any drill stand having a Euro-norm sleeve, thus converting the router to a stand drill and increasing its range of uses. The springs of the plunging mechanism are a little over-strong on this machine, but it is equal to most tasks which the serious amateur woodworker is likely to give it.

Cutting a tenon

100

46 Porter Cable Router 100

47 Porter Cable Router 630

The Euro-norm is a standard set up by manufacturers of power tools in Europe to ensure interchangeability of tools and accessories. Where problems arise in fitting, some manufacturers offer additional sleeves having the 43mm Euro-norm internally and an outside diameter to fit a particular drill stand at attachment (Fig 45).

Makita have the 3608B in this range and this model has been dealt with previously.

The Porter Cable Company offer the Model 100 and this is rated as a 6.5 amp motor, and has a 20,000 rpm no-load speed. The motor is 7/8 hp with high torque power. The depth setting has micrometer adjustment by means of a ring.

The 630 is similar in features but has a 1 hp motor.

HOME CRAFTSMAN ROUTERS

A compact, low-weight router is the Elu 96; I have used one for the past twelve years with no problems.

It has a motor input of 600 watts and an output of 380 watts; a no-load speed of 24,000 rpm and is available in 115 volts and 220 volts. The router weighs 2.7kg (6lb) and has a two-column precision guide for the router base, enabling careful control when plunging. The total enclosure of the springs protects against dirt and working dust. The router base has one pair of opposite sides straight and parallel and is plastic-coated for ease of movement over the work piece. It is fitted with a three-position turret which speeds up repetition work.

This range also includes the 96E which has all the main features of the 96, but in addition, its input is raised to 750 watts with an output of 520 watts. Just 0.1kg (.2lb) heavier, it has a speed range of 8,000 to 24,000 rpm. With the same features as its bigger brother the 177E, it's the luxury job for the man who has a little extra to spend on his first buy.

The plunge stroke on both machines is 50mm (2in); the collet capacity is 6.35mm (1/4in), with optional capacities for 6 and 8mm. Maximum cutter

48 Elu Router No. 96

size is 32mm (1¼in). Both machines are supplied with a 17mm (⅝in) guide bush and spanners to suit the chuck.

Ryobi of Hiroshima in Japan market a number of routers suitable for both the home craftsman and the professional. The 150 is classified by its name – the 'Handy' router; it's a plunge router with a compact and quite powerful unit, and a full range of accessories is available. Input at 750 watts is adequate, and the machine motors well at 24,000 rpm. It has a sliding depth stop and three-stage turret.

A very popular woodworker router is seen in the Black & Decker BD66. It's a plunge action job with an input wattage of 480, no-load speed of 26,000 rpm, and a collet accepting 6.35mm (¼in) cutters.

49 Ryobi Router No. R–150

A neat calibrated depth-stop records depths to a full 51mm (2in) plunge. The knob-type handles are of good size and the carrier to which the straight and curved fences can be fitted, and also the circle guide, are micro-adjustable. It is fitted with a safety knock-off switch which automatically turns the motor off when the machine is inverted on its top. Another feature which is an added advantage is that the motor unit is detachable, giving easy access to the chuck, and at the same time the motor could be attached to a drill or similar stand having a Euro-norm collar size. It's a good looking bargain for the home craftsman.

Bosch of West Germany have two routers, one of which (the POF52) has a detachable motor unit, similar to the DN66 made by Black & Decker, making it an extremely versatile machine. This router has a power input of 500 watts and a no-load speed of 27,000 rpm. The collet accepts 6.35mm (¼in) cutters, and the plunge depth is 52mm (2in). The base has an anti-stick coating, and a full range of accessories is available.

50 Black & Decker BD66 Router
51 Black & Decker BD66 Router with all accessories

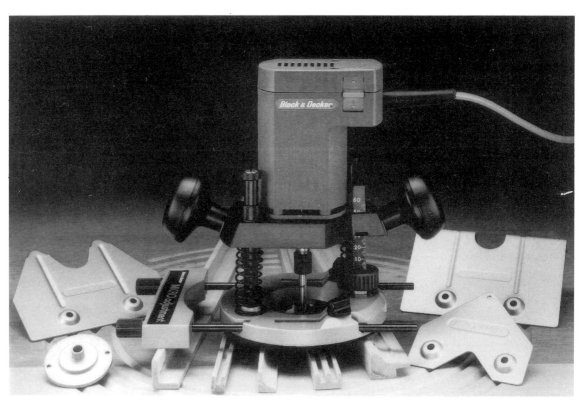

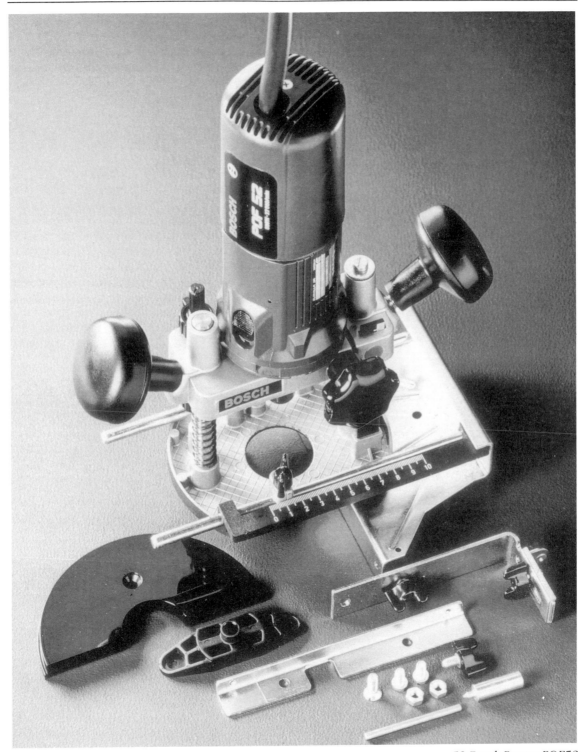

52 Bosch Router POF52

53 Bosch Router POF400

The POF400 has a power rating of 400 watts input, and a no-load speed of 27,000 rpm. The collet accepts 6.35mm (¼in) cutters, and plunges to 48mm (1⅞in). A twist-knob controls and retains the plunge, the other knob being an integral part of the casing.

INVERTED PIN ROUTERS

When attached to a router table so that the cutter projects upward, the router can be referred to as an 'inverted' router. There are a number of purpose-designed inverted routers for the professional and those made by C. R. Onsrud of Troutman, North Carolina are excellent examples of the type. Their model 2003 has a cast-iron machine frame and spindle mountings, and it is set on a welded supporting base which is insulated against noise. Its throat capacity is 508mm (20in), and the table measures 610mm by 914mm (24in by 36in). The router is fitted with a 3½hp motor which is single-phase 120 volt.

54 Onsrud overhead pin router

55 Micom sign-carving and copy routing machine

Simple templates give the possibility of making complicated shapes using internal cut-outs, slotting, boring, mortice cuts and shaping. A sample part can be reproduced by using it as a jig and tracing round it with the overhead guide pin. This can be done on a direct one-to-one ratio, the pin diameter can be offset to increase or decrease the part size. The machine has three quick-change guide pins of 6.35mm (¼in), 9.25mm (⅜in) and 12.7mm (½in) size. Master templates can be made of thin plywood, hardboard or even cardboard of sufficient strength to prevent the pin running over the edge. Toughened material, of which Tufnol is a well known example would be ideal for templates in continual use. Patterns can be made up by pinning additional pieces to the existing pattern material. The

guide pin runs against the pinned-on pieces, while the router cutter makes a smooth continuous cut in the pattern stock. It is possible to do freehand work, routing to a pencil line with the top mounted guide pin being used as a pointer. Every template can be made on the router, and the variations are limitless. There are quite a number of machines similar in design and work pattern from this company.

Micom sign-carving and copy routing machine
This is an interesting machine having a 1:1 fixed ratio pantograph. The router and stylus are mounted on the pantograph; the stylus is free to move across the copy table on which the master template, which acts

56 Examples of work from the Micom

as the copy, is cramped – using side rails and end cramps. Below the router is the universal work holding fixture in which the work piece is cramped. The work-holding fixture consists of two dovetail-section rails with two movable cramping blocks, and two plastic cramp jaws which can be cut to hold irregular shapes. Any length of work piece can be produced by working in sections; the machine area is approximately 380mm by 230mm (15in by 9in) with a maximum work piece height of 127mm (5in).

The machine will accept the Bosch 52, the Elu 96 and the 96E with standard 6.35mm (¼in) collets. A wide range of accessories is available, including a number of styles of numerals and alphabets. Incised and relief lettering is available and greater opportunities are afforded the cabinet maker and pattern maker. The company also markets a number of specialist engraving machines.

ROUTER ACCESSORIES

There is a number of very useful accessories which can be obtained for the router, and they serve to assist in the attainment of perfection, or make the handling of the router easier.

57 Elu universal sub-base with handles

Universal sub-base

This consists of a flat base sheet which is fitted with two handles for extra control; it is easily fitted to most routers. A tracking kit can also be added to the base.

Tracking kit

This consists of a tracking plate which can be attached to the fence arms of the router. The plate slides in a groove which may be in the job itself or in a wooden strip cramped alongside the work piece. It affords perfect, fool-proof control where accurate straight-line movement is essential. As mentioned above, it can be fitted to the universal sub-base.

Circular sub-base

When fitted to the router, it enables cutting to be carried out at a fixed distance from a template regardless of the angle of the router. Trend guide bushes fit into the centre of the base.

59 Elu circular sub-base

Stepped base and follower assembly

This is designed for laminate trimming. The fence-roller is set at a depth to suit the thickness of the timber. The stepped base allows the router cutter to be set to exact laminate thickness.

Table accessory kit

This kit could well appear in the router table section, since when made up it does indeed serve as a router table. The kit converts the Elu 96 and Elu 96E into miniature spindle moulders.

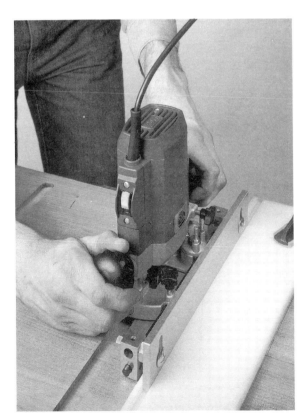

58 Elu tracking kit

60 Accessory kit table with feet screwed to a board for holding with the bench dogs

It consists of a table to which four legs can be fitted which give sufficient height from the table to clear the router. Clips can be used to attach these legs to a piece of blockboard, which can in turn be secured on the bench top, using bench dogs. It has two pressure cramps; one can be secured to the very deep fence, and the other to a bracket which slides along the edge of the table like a fence. Both these cramps are sprung and can be finely adjusted. A copy roller can also be added for profiling and the legs can be removed for bench mounting the router in the horizontal position.

Fine fence adjusters
These give fine adjustment to the fence over its entire adjustment range, and are an ideal addition for most grooving and moulding operations.

Fine height adjuster
A short-reach adjuster is ideal where adjustments are made over a comparatively short range. Particularly when using a dovetail jig.

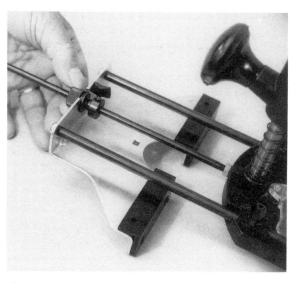

61 Fine fence adjuster

62 Elu baseplate extension

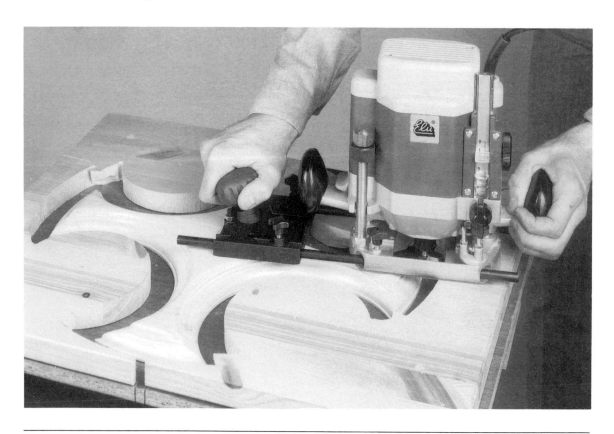

Fine height adjuster

This is ideal when using a dovetail attachment, or other work where fine adjustments have to be made, over a fairly long range to ensure close fitting.

Elu base-plate extension

This extension slides on to the fence arms to provide additional support and stability, particularly when some of the groundwork has already been removed. A very useful addition is the provision of an adjustable pointed pin for radius or circle cutting. The extension can also be fitted with a trimming plate for the vertical flush-cutting of laminates.

Elu edge trimming accessory

Where a great deal of edge trimming of laminates is to be carried out, the edge trimming attachment which slides over the fence arms makes a good investment.

64 Elu MKF67 Edge Trimmer

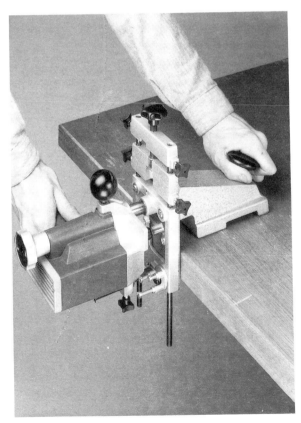

63 Edge trimming accessory fitted to the MOF69

Laminate trimmers

These are specialist tools, particularly important for a workshop which carries out a great deal of kitchen-fitting work where plastic laminates are widely used. For the serious home craftsman and the small production shop, the fitting of a special base to the normal router will suffice. Whichever style of router is in use, only those cutters specified as suitable for cutting laminates should be fitted.

The Elu MKF67 is typical of this type of tool. Separate accessories are available to cater for almost every conceivable laminate trimming problem, from the straightforward trimmer base, through offset and tilt, to two separate sub-bases for trim and tilt. It is fitted with a 6.35mm (¼in) collet.

A – UK

Make	Model	rpm	Motor input watts	output watts	Collet sizes	Depth, type of Adjustment and depth of plunge	Type of switch	Type of handle	Voltage
Elu	96	24,000	600	340	¼ (6, 8mm)	Plunge 50mm (2in)	Slider	Knobs	240 or 115
	96E	8,000 to 24,000	750	520	¼ (6, 8mm)	Plunge 50mm (2in)	Slider	Knobs	
	177 (3337 in USA)	20,000	1600	960	¼, ½, (6, 8, 10 & 12mm)	Plunge 62mm (2⁷⁄₁₆in)	Slider	Knobs	
	177E (3338 in USA)	8,000 to 20,000	1850	1100	¼, ½ (6, 8, 10 & 12mm)	Plunge 62mm (2⁷⁄₁₆in)	Slider	Knobs	
	131	22,000	1300	750	¼ (6, 8, 10 & 12mm)	Plunge 62mm (2⁷⁄₁₆in)	Slider	Knobs	
Black & Decker DIY	BD66	26,000	480		¼	Plunge 50mm (2in)	Slider	Knobs	240
	SR100	24,000	600		¼	Plunge 50mm (2in)	Slider	Knobs	240
Bosch Professional	1601	25,000	780		¼	Spiral	Trigger	Knobs	240 or 110
	1603	25,000	1000		¼	Spiral	Trigger	D-handle and knob	
	1604	25,000	1150		¼, ½	Spiral	Toggle	Knobs	
Home Craftsman	POF 52	27,000	320		¼	Plunge 52mm (2¹⁄₁₆in)	Slider	Knobs	240 or 110
	POF 400	27,000	400		¼	Plunge 48mm (1⁷⁄₈in)	Slider	Knobs	240
Makita	3608B	23,000	500		¼, ³⁄₈	Ring	Trigger	Arms	240 or 110
	3600B	22,000	1500		¼, ³⁄₈	Plunge	Toggle	Knobs	
	3601B	23,000	930		¼, ³⁄₈	Ring	Trigger	D-handle and knobs	
	3612BR	23,000	1600		½	Plunge 65mm (2⁹⁄₁₆in)	Slider	Knobs	240
Hitachi	FM8	27,000	550		¼ (6 & 8mm)	Plunge 52mm (2¹⁄₁₆in)	Slider	Knobs	240 or 110
	TR12	22,000	1300		½	Plunge 52mm (2¹⁄₁₆in)	Slider	Knobs	
Kress	6900	27,000	450	250		Plunge 46mm (1¹³⁄₁₆in)	Slider	Knobs	220 or 110
	6900E	8 to 24,000	600	350	¼ (6mm)	Plunge 46mm (1¹³⁄₁₆in)	Slider	Knobs	240 or 110
Ryobi	R150	24,000	750/1hp		8mm	Plunge 50mm (2in)	Slider	Knobs	240 or 110
	R500	22,000	1,500/2hp		½/12mm	Plunge 60mm (2³⁄₈in)	Slider	Knobs	240 or 110
	R330	24,000	1,400/2hp		½/12mm	Spiral 20mm (1³⁄₄in)	Push	Two arms	240 or 110
	R331	24,000	1,400/2hp		½/12mm	Spiral 20mm (³⁄₄in)	Trigger	D-handle and knob	240 or 110

B – USA

Black & Decker Professional	3310	25,000	1½	¼in	Rack	Toggle	Knob
	3335	18,000	3½	¼, ⅜, ½in	Ring	Toggle	Two arms
Black & Decker Consumer	7600	30,000	⅝	¼in	Ring	Slider	Two arms
	7604	30,000	¾	¼in	Ring	Slider	Two arms
	7613	25,000	1	¼in	Rack	Trigger	Two arms
	7614	25,000	1½	¼in	Rack	Trigger	Two arms
	7615	25,000	1½	¼in	Rack and Plunge	Trigger	Two arms
	7666	25,000	1½	¼in	Rack and Plunge	Trigger	Two arms
Milwaukee	5620	23,000	1	¼in and ⅜in	Ring	Slider	Knobs
	5660	24,500	1½	¼, ⅜, ½in	Ring	Slider	Knobs
	5680	26,000	2	¼, ⅜, ½in	Ring	Slider	Knobs
Sears	1730	25,000	⅝	¼in	Ring	Slider	Arms
	1755	25,000	1	¼in	Ring	Slider	Knobs
	1756	25,000	1¼	¼in	Ring	Slider	Knobs
	1743	25,000	1½	¼in	Ring	Slider	Knobs
	1749	25,000	variable	¼in	Ring	Trigger	Knobs
	1750	11,000 to 25,000	variable	¼in	Ring	Trigger	Knobs
Porter Cable	100	22,000	⅞	¼in	Spiral	Toggle	Knobs
	630	22,000	1	¼in	Spiral	Toggle	Knobs
	690	22,000	1½	¼in	Spiral	Toggle	Knobs
	691	22,000	1½	½in	Spiral	Toggle	D-handle & knobs
	536	23,000	1½	¼in, ½in	Spiral	Toggle	Knobs
	537	23,000	1½	¼in, ½in	Spiral	Trigger	D-handle & knobs
	518	10 to 22,000	3	¼in, ½in	Spiral	Trigger	D-handle & knobs
	520	10,000 to 22,000	3	¼in, ½in	Spiral	Trigger	D-handles

NB Collets will only accept router cutters with shanks of exact size. Any attempt to insert other sizes will either be found impossible or result in distortion of the collet jaws with the cutter running out of centre.

Manufacturers having standard sizes in metric collets offer optional Imperial.

Horsepower quoted is a close approximation.

All USA routers are quoted as 110 volt

5 How to Handle the Router

Of all the power tools, the router is probably the easiest to learn to use and, when under control, it gives the most satisfying results.

Before commencing to use it, check that the power supply is correct for the router motor and confirm it carefully with the name plate found on most tools. Ensure also that the power supply in the workshop is adequate to serve the router, and that the source has the correct fuse capacity.

Choose the router cutter to suit the particular cut to be made, and be quite sure that its shank size matches that of the router's collet. Make a choice also in the type of cutter – as already mentioned, HSS for timber generally and TCT for man-made boards and the like.

Remove the plug from the power source and check the power cable for flaws before commencing to set up or adjust the machine. If the working area is at a greater distance from the source of supply than the machine cable will allow, an extension cord must be used. Be certain that it is rated correctly, don't have it overlong, and don't use it in the coiled or partially coiled state since this can be dangerous.

Clear the bench of surplus gear and secure the timber to be worked upon by one or other of the suggested methods (see Chapter 8).

Use of the collet

The collet is attached to the motor spindle and is needed to hold the router cutters firmly and centrally in place. It must always be kept in perfect condition.

To clamp a cutter in place, simply hold the motor spindle with the spanner included with the router, and tighten down with the other spanner to secure the clamping nut. Some routers use a steel pin fitted to hold the spindle while turning the clamping nut.

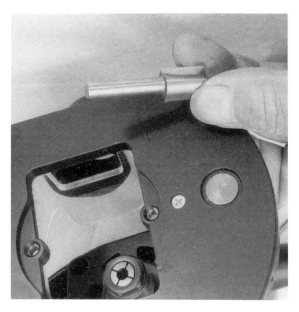

65 Fitting the router bit – the collet and bit

66 Router collet – jaw components

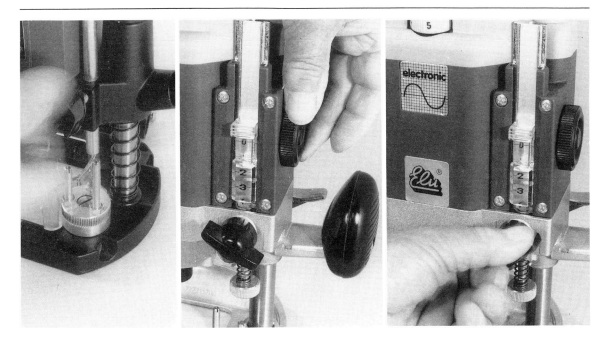

To remove the cutter, release the collet first, by turning the clamping nut – once again using both spanners, or the steel pin and spanner. Then, after a few more turns, remove the router cutter. The clamping nut and the collet must always be flush at the front end; if this is not so, remove both components from the machine, and push the collet into the clamping nut so that it engages fully and the jaws come up flush with the front end of the clamping nut. Failure to do this could result in it being virtually impossible to remove a cutter. The method of setting up the collet must be followed when making a change of collet size or replacing it.

Some collets have two stages of tightening as, for example, the Elu 96. Be sure to complete both stages, remove the spanners and place them in a safe place away from the action.

Always make certain that the cutter shank is in-

(left) 67 Setting the depth rod; (centre) 68 Elu 177 depth-setting knob; (right) 69 Locking the depth setting

serted fully into the collet chuck, then withdraw it a fraction before securing. Failure to insert the cutter shank properly is dangerous and will result in collet wear. To remove the cutter, reverse the sequence. Always store the cutters in small wooden racks or cases – never drop them loosely into a box.

To set the cutting depth, loosen the holding knob first, then bring down the cutter so that it just touches the surface of the work piece. Tighten down on the holding knob and loosen the depth-stop screw – this permits the depth rod to drop on to one of the three registers of the anvil if one is fitted (if not, then the depth rod will register against a stop on the base).

70 Depth stop used in conjunction with the turret for progressive routing to depth

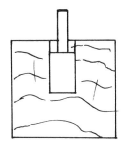
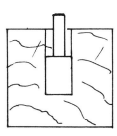
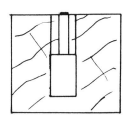

Reference to the scale provided either on the stop itself, or on the body, will show a reading. Now raise the rod by an amount equal to the depth required and tighten down on the depth-rod screw to hold the setting. Loosen the holding knob once again and the router will be ready for use.

The three possible settings on the turret will be most useful when cutting depths which require to be altered during a particular operation which uses the same cutter throughout the work, or whenever stage-cutting a deep recess using one particular cutter for the whole job. Check the setting by pushing down on the router and reading the actual cutter depth on the edge of the work piece. A number of machines use a different setting device – that on the Hitachi uses a rod, but a screwed rod with nuts serves as a micrometer adjustment. Provision is also made to lock a particular setting for repetition work. The fixed setting screws on the turret device almost always have locking nuts which should be secured before commencing a cut, since a slightly loose nut can vibrate further and alter the depth of the cut with disastrous results.

Many router manufacturers offer a precision depth adjuster as an optional extra, and this fits into the depth-stop housing in the body. To use this device, remove the standard depth-rod, screw down on one of the three turret stops, and slightly tighten the adjusting screw. Precision setting can then be obtained by turning on the precision setting-rod knob.

71 Micrometer adjustment – top left
*   Turret – bottom right*

72 Placing the fence on the arms

73 Fitting the fence

74 Setting the fence with the rule

GUIDE SETTINGS

In order to ensure accurate movement of the router when cutting, a fence must be used. For straight cutting of grooves and rebates all routers are supplied with a straight fence, which is fitted with two fence arms which slide into holes on the top of the base. It can then be secured in any set position by screwing down the wing nuts. The better class of routers have small springs or spring washers located under the nuts to prevent them from vibrating loose. Great inaccuracy with some danger as well can be the result if the fence becomes slack. Using a rule, set the fence at the required distance from the cutter and tighten down the nuts. Some machines have a fine-setting device which can give much greater accuracy. Always check the alignment of the fence after setting.

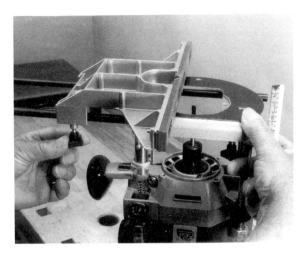

75 Fixing the fence

When copying has to be done a profile is made from plywood or similar material. This is used in conjunction with a guide bush which is secured to the base of the router with screws, and at least one of these is usually provided with the machine. Additional guides in a wide range of sizes are available. Cutters provided with a guide pin permit the use of the router without the fence; the guide pin consists of a rounded pin at the lower extremity of the cutter. The guide pin runs against the edge of the work piece and thus controls the cutting.

Many cutters are fitted with an extension of this device, namely a ball bearing replacing the guide pin. This eliminates the tendency of the guide pin to burn the timber, which does sometimes happen when the progress of the router cutting is slowed for some reason.

76 Fitting a guide bush

When making the profiles, accurate measurements must be made to ensure perfect sizing. Refer to the line drawing and you will note that if the template is used on the inside, the dimensions of the finished job will be less than the dimension of the template by an amount equal to the measurement at 'A', that is, the distance between the edge of the template and the edge of the cutter. If the outside of the template is used the reverse is the case. See page 99 for details. When using templates be sure to adequately secure them with double-sided adhesive tape, or hotmelt glue, or small veneer pins.

77 Router cutter with fixed pilot

When following a curved path, most routers are provided with a curved path guide which is fitted to the normal fence. These have a ball-bearing roller

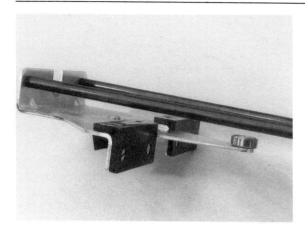

78 Profile fence for curved work

80 Kress router with trammel fitted

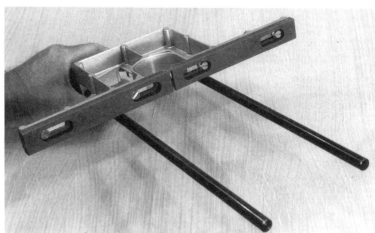

79 Elu 177 fence

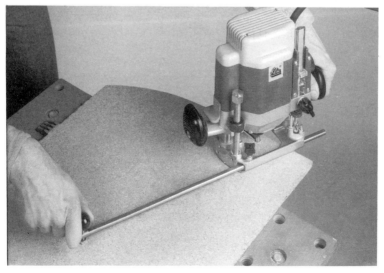

81 Trammel bar in use

and will permit the router to move in any path dictated by a guide or template.

Trimming thin boards can present a problem, particularly if they are faced with a plastic laminate. A number of fences are fitted with an angled face which is covered with a plastic laminate, and this can be removed and re-set to provide a close contact to the fence.

For cutting circular work, routers can be fitted with a trammel bar. This can be inserted into one of the fence arm holes in the router base. A pin on the trammel bar locates into a tiny hole at the centre of the circle and ensures accuracy.

After all adjustments have been made, plug the router into the power outlet. Check that the motor is in its released position; that is, at the topmost position of its travel. Press the switch, allow the motor to reach maximum revolutions before carefully plunging to the cutting position. With very deep cuts it is as well to take several shallow cuts; this will reduce the wear on the router and on the cutter, as the latter can break if too great a cut is taken. Twist the holding knob to secure the chosen depth, or use the lever lock, and move the router along the line of cut, being sure to check that it is being fed in the opposing direction to that in which the cutter is rotating. The line drawing illustrates the rotation of the cutter in relation to the forward movement of the router. Concentrate on keeping the fence or the guide close to the edge of the timber and all will be well. When plunging, move the router forward immediately full depth has been reached to eliminate any possibility of burning caused by friction. SLOW MOVEMENT RESULTS IN BURNING; FAST MOVEMENT IN OVER-LOADING.

After completing the cut stop the machine and return the cutter to its highest position by releasing the knob, lay it down on its side just in case you have forgotten TO SWITCH OFF, OR THE CUTTER IS

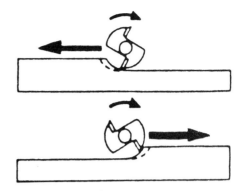

82 Up-cutting and down-cutting

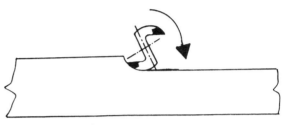

83 Direction of rotation

STILL ROTATING. This is also of great importance when a guide is in position as it might get damaged; a dent or burr caused by striking another metal object may cause the guide to deviate when in use. It is also vital to preserve the quality of finish on the base of the router to ensure its easy movement along the work piece, and to avoid scratching.

NEVER tighten down on the collet clamping nut if a cutter has not been inserted otherwise the collet could be damaged. Note: the jaws are held in place with a strong spring, and consequently a little effort will have to be applied to remove the jaws and insert the new ones. If a guard is provided, use it; keep your fingers away from the cutter at all times even when the router isn't plugged in.

6 Holding the Work

The work must be securely held at all times, both for the safety of personnel and also for the job itself. With the cutter revolving at such high speed, a work piece held insecurely can leave the bench, with disastrous results.

Battens and small pieces can be held in the normal woodworking vice, taking care to ensure that the cutter will clear both the bench top and the vice when running. Alternatively, use the dogs set in the tail-vice and the bench top.

85 Record Spingrip G-cramp

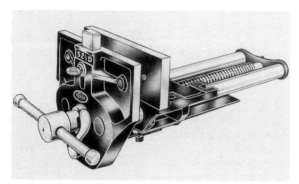

84 Dog vice

Flat boards of small size can be held adequately with double-sided adhesive tape. The basic requirement here is to have a flat, flush top to work on, and both bench top and the work piece must be free from dust. This is an amazingly strong method, and one I have used for many years. Always take care when removing the tape since it has a tremendous grip and can bring slivers of timber with it.

Large boards can be held between the dogs on the bench top, but if this cannot be done then G-cramps can be used. Small boards can be secured using hot-melt glue. Several spots of glue are placed on the bench top and the board is pressed down firmly on them. A knife slipped between will release the work when it is finished. Should any difficulty arise, the glue can be softened with an electric paint stripper, or, alternatively, the knife can be warmed. A warm

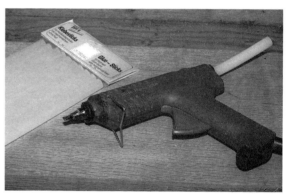

86 Hot-melt gun and glue sticks

knife can of course be used to remove any glue from the bench top.

Boards can also be held with bench holdfasts. There are several types, and if the bench top has two locations this method will be found useful as the holdfast will not interfere with the path of the router.

Small panels can be worked on by placing them in a small frame and using folding wedges to hold them in position. This method provides a means of holding a completed panel without any chance of damage or bruising from vice jaws and the like.

87 Sloberg bench showing holdfast

88 Sloberg holdfast

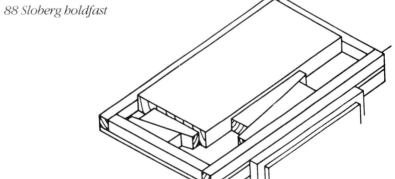

89 Panel held in folding wedge board

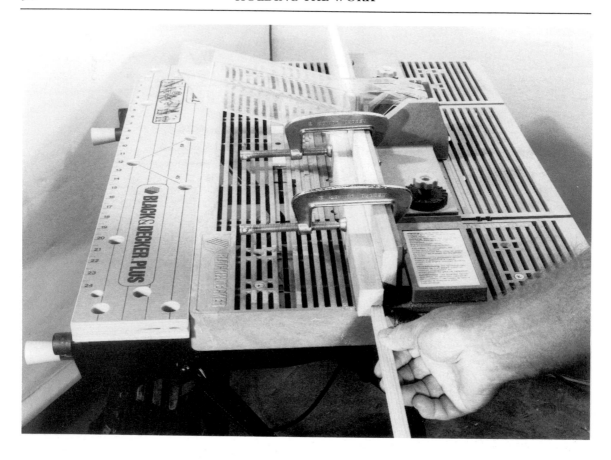

*90 Passing the material through a tunnel cramped to
the fence*

91 Pattern box

With very large flat panels a similar arrangement can be set up, using the bench top with strips fastened on with pins or cramps to provide upstands against which the wedges can bear.

When working with small-section strip material, the router is best set up in a router table. A prepared piece of wood is fitted to the table against the fence to form a tunnel through which the strips are passed to the cutter. This removes any possibility of the fingers being too close to the rotating cutter, and also reduces chatter.

Those woodworkers who have a Black & Decker Workmate can use either the built-in vice which forms the top, or for wider work, fit the dogs into the holes provided and set the work piece up between them. See Fig 13 page 15.

For repetition work any number of box arrangements can be made. These can have the master pattern fitted with a hinge, and folding wedges can be pressed into use to hold the work piece underneath.

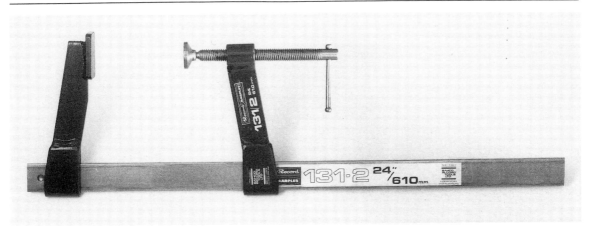

92 Long-reach cramps

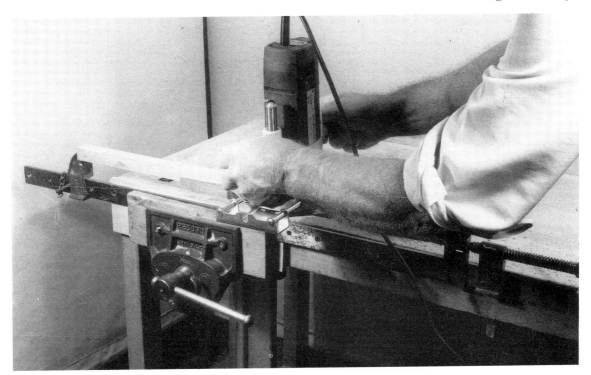

93 Long small-section material held in a sash cramp.

In joint making it may be necessary to secure several rails or stiles together temporarily while exact cuts are made. Such jobs need the use of quick-acting cramps used in pairs.

When long timbers have to be worked upon they may be too long to be supported adequately in a vice which is fitted to the side of the bench. This can be overcome by using a long sash cramp which, in turn, is held in the vice.

Holding curved panels

This is often a problem when working with several kinds of tool, as the traditional English bench with its vice fitted on the side towards one end makes the job difficult. A bench having two rows of dogs is probably the best way to hold round or unevenly edged material.

A flat piece of board can provide a good solution. It is fitted with two or three round pegs or studs close to one edge, and then plain blocks of wood are screwed in place opposite the pegs to hold the work. They must not, of course, stand as high as the panel being routed. Small cam levers can be substituted for the wooden blocks.

Folding wedge vice for small panels

Again, a piece of flat board is used and two strips of timber screwed along both long sides close to the edges. These strips must be thinner than the panel to be cut, which is placed between the strips and held in place by tapping a pair of folding wedges in place at either end. The board itself can be held between bench dogs; but if the bench is not fitted with dogs, a length of timber screwed underneath close to the forward edge will serve to secure the piece in the vice.

94 Curved work held with pegs and blocks

95 A folding wedge vice

96 Cramping board holding a panel for fielding

97 Flat board with screwed blocks

Holding fielded panels

This can be a real problem, particularly if heavy cutting is to be carried out. Many years ago I used the system shown in the photograph to hold a book for gluing the edges in the days when I indulged in the art of bookbinding. The assembly consists of a board bored to receive a pair of coachbolts which, in turn, penetrate a cramping strip and hold it in place by means of wing-nuts. The panel to be routed is placed between the cramping strip and the board, and screwing down on the wing-nuts secures the panel in place. A strip can be glued to the underside of the board to enable it to be held in the vice.

Flat board

This is simply a piece of flat board with a strip of timber glued to the underside by which it can be held in the vice. This will be found useful where a really flat-topped bench is not available, or where the bench or work-top may not provide a suitable surface for double-sided adhesive tape or hot-melt glue to be used. The device can also be used with small wooden blocks screwed on to secure the work, and this is most useful where the edge of the job is curved or shaped in any way.

Vacuum cramping

Holding a work piece can often present difficulties, as most of the holding methods already described will tend to obstruct the free movement of the router. In most cases, any marking of the work piece must be avoided, and screw or pin holes resulting from efforts to hold the work while it is being routed will be abhorrent to a craftsman.

In small production work – or even in the serious home craftsman's workshop – a small vacuum system may well be worth the expense involved. Many people have doubts about the efficiency of vacuum systems, yet they have been in use over a long period in industry.

A small vacuum pump with an exhaust displacement of 17 psi (lb per square inch) is perfect for the making of a vacuum suction pad at least 305mm (12in) square.

Vacuum equipment is available to make up a suction pad, but adequate calculations need to be made as to the size and type of work to be held before any purchases are made. The work being held must be well supported to avoid distortion, but at the same time the support must not reduce the vacuum exhaust so that its holding power is seriously impaired, and this means that the pad must be carefully designed.

The sealant Neoprene material to contain the vacuum can be obtained in strip or sheet form – it should be between 1.5 and 2.5mm thick, and of the close-cell variety. Using thicker material may result in vibration, with a resultant poor finish on the work

piece. The Neoprene strip is self-adhesive, and it can be overlapped and glued and cut with a finely sharpened knife. A vented hole in the body of the pad can be cut in any convenient place. If support for the work is needed within the pad, small blocks can be cut from Neoprene.

This method is ideal for use with overhead routers; but it can be used also for holding a work piece down, for working with the router inverted, and when using the router as a spindle moulder. In this case, the work piece template is converted into a vacuum pad by attaching the Neoprene sheet to it, and the template should be made from a hard material such as Perspex, PVC, or Tufnol.

7 Router Tables

The growth in the development of portable power tools has encouraged manufacturers to increase their versatility by designing benches to accommodate the various types and thus convert them into table-tools. The router has proved its capabilities as a hand-held tool, but many users have been quick to assess its possibilities and have converted them to act as spindle moulders by attaching them underneath home-made tables. I did this many years ago with one of the early Black & Decker routers which had a rack-and-pinion type mechanism for depth-setting.

This table was made from square Speedframe material with a top of sheet steel. Complete with fence, it has helped in the refurbishing of two homes and many hundreds of feet of material have been passed through it.

One of the most popular pieces of equipment to have been developed in recent years is the Black & Decker Workmate – I'd like ten pence for each one sold to date! The uses to which the Workmate has been put are legion, and it is therefore not surprising

98 Black & Decker Workmate 2

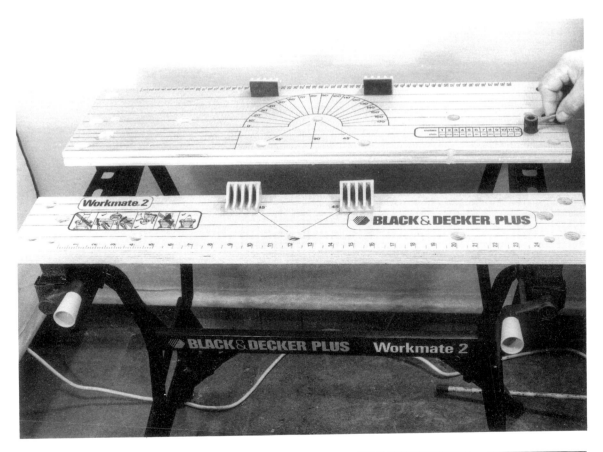

99 Workmate 2 fitted with power table and folded
   for storing

101 Wooden fence facings fitted

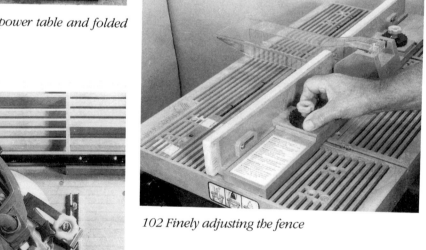

102 Finely adjusting the fence

100 Elu 96 router secured on the table underside

103 Mitre fence in use

to see the launch of the Workcentre. This fits on to the new Workmate 2 work bench. It comes complete with a split fence with fine adjustment to both parts, and has adequate cramping facilities. The guards seem a little big but are fine for the job. Much plastic is used in its construction but for the home user it would seem quite durable. Black & Decker routers, plus the Elu and the Bosch, can be easily assembled to it.

The Dunlop Powerbase

This comprises a folding bench made of metal, with a 25mm (1in) thick top; the top has a centre portion which can be removed for the insertion of several power tools. The router can be mounted on top, or underneath to act as a spindle moulder. The Powerbase has a splendid long fence which comes into use when the router is in the inverted position. The fence cramps are adjustable and can be used to hold the work. The router can be used in the overhead position in conjunction with two runners which run the full width of the table, and which can be cramped securely in place; this simplifies the cutting of housings and the making of cuts across wide boards. The table itself is what you buy; most of the attachments come as extras, and this includes the router kit. Any

104 Dunlop Powerbase

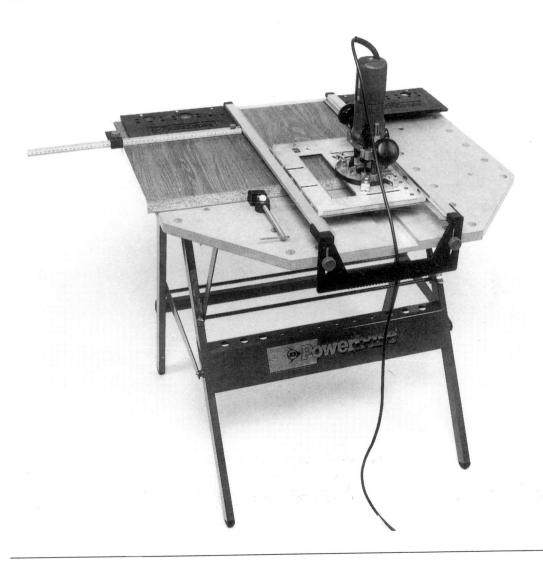

105 Powerbase – Bosch router at work

106 Skilten Skilmate

electrical switching is also an extra. It's a good work-table and those woodworkers who have little space but a full complement of power tools will be pleased with it.

Skilten Skilmate
Comprises a straightforward bench top which is composed of thick plywood, sitting on a steel frame. Unlike the Black & Decker Workmate, this one doesn't also serve as a vice. The legs can be adjusted, indeed, this is a feature which enables the table to serve also as a drawing board. The router fits a tool plate which itself drops down into a recessed portion of the table, revealed when the opening section is dropped down. The router plate comes as an extra to the table, as do the fence and fittings. The Skilmate has no guards, but these may well appear later.

Meritcraft Powermate

This is a short-legged bench-top table cast in aluminium alloy; it can be purchased with a work-stand as an extra. The router fits to a plate for attachment to the table. A small fence is provided but the manufacturers haven't fitted a guard. The small table size makes it adequate for the home worker.

Triton

This is a very impressive piece of equipment and one which I shall be reluctant to lose from my workshop. Designed by an Australian, it has been the subject of close scrutiny by the makers since it left the drawing board, and such care shows. The table is quite different from all others inasmuch as it is of box-like construction, open-sided. The top is fitted with sliding aluminium tracks at both long sides, and each of two carriages slide along them. The router carriage permits the assembly of any number of standard routers. When the router is used in the overhead position, the top table slides underneath to serve as a support for the work piece. The top can be adjusted to accommodate different thicknesses of material. To convert to a spindle moulder, the carriage slides to one end of the rail and flips over to slide back into the working position; a router table then fits over the top, and to this can be fitted very sound fences and safety guards.

The main table can be fitted with an underframe which is most sturdy and easy to put together; and

108 Router fitted to the sliding table

this can be fitted with a set of wheels – so useful when one gets to be as old and decrepit as this author! One of the very best ideas is the electric switching. The router is plugged into a socket on the underframe; this socket also houses the switch which is of the tumbler type, but a flap is hinged over it which knocks off the switch if touched with the hand or knee – a super-safety feature. The carriages slide on nylon bearings, and the tolerances are indeed close. The router will fit into the standard carriage (which was designed, I guess, for the saws), but unfortunately you lose out a little in depth of cut, so it's best to get the router kit.

107 Triton Workcentre – the front showing table height adjustment and switch

109 Triton – switch plate to plug in the router

110 Bringing the router to the overhead position

111 Router in position

112 Fitting the sliding table

113 Positioning the router table

114 Router table showing side fixing

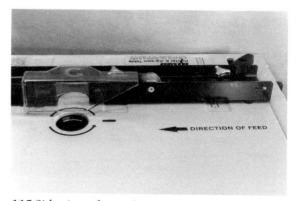

115 Side view of guard

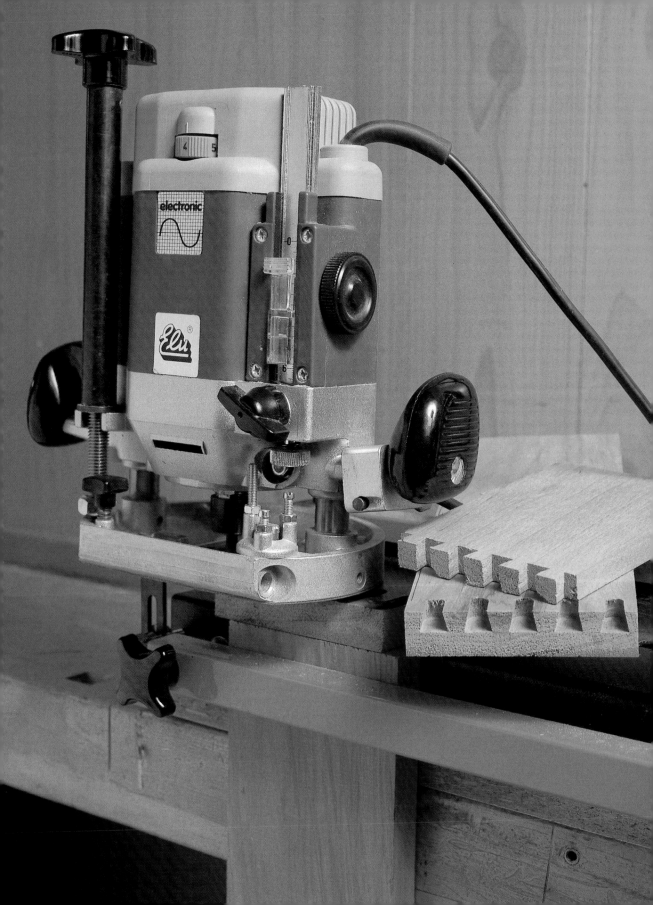

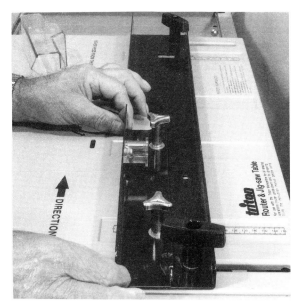

116 Fine setting the fence

The instruction book is excellent. A video tape made by the originators of the machine is also available, and this oozes confidence and underlines the perfection of the machine. My first test was to make a bookcase and the only addition I had to make was a stop to limit the length of the housings and this was attached to a sub-table made in plywood. The lower table was set up, using the calibrations which are clearly and accurately marked at both ends of the box. The locks which hold the tables securely in place seem foolproof. Certainly, it cannot be used as a general work bench like the Workmate, but it can eliminate the need for a table saw, a jig saw and a spindle moulder. The cost should therefore take into account the saving in not having to buy these machines. In the end, one also saves a good deal on floor space, which must be a bonus for many woodworkers.

A work station with a difference
When the router is held in the stationary position one tends to think of router tables where generally the router is attached underneath the table, in effect converting it into a simple shaper. The Triton work table (see page 65) is singularly different, inasmuch as it can be used with the router in both modes – above and below.

Problems arise when it comes to angled cutting with any of the tables, and the designing of a jig is usually the answer. There is however a solution; the Wolfcraft Electronic drill stand. It is a very versatile work centre for the woodworker, with drilling and routing in the vertical plane, or at any angle between the horizontal and the vertical; there are also innumerable metal machining operations as an added feature.

It comprises a basic table to which can be attached a column which houses the machine head. This machine head has a Euro-norm sleeve which will accept a number of the well known brands of routers and drills as well as those made by Wolfcraft themselves. An adaptor can be inserted in the base to permit the assembly of a more normal drill-stand column – indeed, one of a different make can be introduced. A very fine machine table which can be continuously adjusted can also be fitted to the base,

117 Wolfcraft Electronic drill stand

Cutting a dovetail

118 Cutting a mortise

and the table is accurately machined to accept an engineer's vice and a number of other useful aids.

But the best is yet to come, and this must really be a 'first' for woodworkers. Every movement can be monitored with LEDs (Light Emitting Diodes), placed so that they can be seen readily and instantly re-positioned if sighting is difficult. Without going into technicalities, one of the most common examples of an LED is the 'read-out' panel on a calculator. The machine head is actuated with a long lever handle, and a hand wheel at the top controls the downward movement. Depth-setting is by a collar alongside the lever. At the topmost position the LED readout can be set at zero and the depth read out in half millimetre (0.002in) steps as the work proceeds.

The router collar can be rotated through 360°, and the head assembly by 90° between horizontal and vertical. The markings here are extremely accurate, and both these features have drop handles to lock the setting. The distance between the face of the

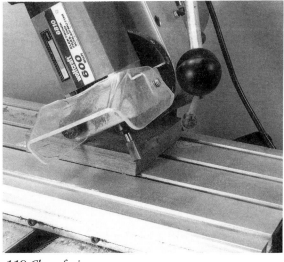

119 Chamfering

column and centre of the cutting tool is 168mm (6⅝in) which is a fair throat for a machine assembly of this kind.

Very good cramping bars, which work in conjunction with the slots in the table and an engineer's vice, make work-holding easy. The table can also be fitted with a fence which is an adequate safety guard while working both straight and curved work. In addition, the machine head has a hinged safety guard which can be used with the machine in most modes.

The unit can be fitted with a Wolfcraft router; the electronic router which I had offered speeds between 8,000 and 24,000 rpm. The Kress Electronic, the Bosch POF52, and the Hitachi – the latter two having been separated from their bases – also fitted perfectly.

I used the unit to cut some haunched mortises shown in the halftones; also to make numerous boring cuts, including the cutting of plugs for inlaying in the clockface seen on page 196.

Drilling and milling stand

To the owners of routers like the Bosch POF52, the Black & Decker DN66, and the Hitachi TR8, the addition of the Bosch S7 drilling and milling stand will be most welcome. Although designed to receive the power drill, it will also accept these three routers, all of which have the 43mm diameter Euro-norm collar.

A small routing and milling bench of 250mm by 600mm (9⅞in by 23⅝in) which has a calibrated scale, parallel fence, and guard can be attached to the drill stand. The versatile craftsman will be able to expand on this to increase its performance.

Luna router table

This table, measuring 650mm by 500mm (25⅝in by 19¹¹/₁₆in), has a height of 350mm (13¾in). It is made in steel with sturdy legs of angled form. The straight fence is made of steel, and there are two pressure guards fitted for safe working; the machine doesn't have a purpose-designed guard as such. Optional extras are: a copying device for curved work; a mitre fence; and a 60mm (2⅜in) suction duct coupling for waste removal. The table is fitted with a no-voltage trip switch and 1.5 metres (5 feet) of cable. An added attraction is an adaptor for the fitting of a jigsaw.

Elu 551 combination bench

This bench has been designed to accommodate both a circular saw and a router assembly, but the kits are

120 Bosch drilling and milling stand

121 Elu 551 bench – both guards in use

quite separate and accessories can be bought to suit.

It consists of an accurately machined cast-aluminium table to which tubular legs are fitted; the legs can easily be removed for transportation or storage. The table is machined to receive a pressure guard and a mitre fence, the former being standard. The fence is cast and carefully designed so that much of the waste leaves the point of the cutter through the right hand side of the fence. A pressure guard is fitted to the fence in a vertical position directly over the cutting point, and an extra one can be placed horizontally to bear against the work piece and hold it firmly up against the fence. Both pressure guards can be accurately positioned by screw adjustment.

A no-volt release switch can be fitted to one of the legs, and the plug for the router is pushed into the underside. Thus, we have instant shut-off of power, and no attachment has to be fitted to the router itself.

All the Elu routers can be fitted. The smaller ones – like the 96 – are mounted by means of the fence arms, but if the 131, 177 or 177E is to be used they are screwed directly into the underside of the table. I experienced only one little difficulty (probably because I'm getting old!); the setting of the plunge required quite an effort because the springs are really strong. (Elu recommend the use of their optional Fine Height Adjuster with this bench.) The fence squares up accurately with the accessory grooves and the measurement scale was accurate.

In use the table was trouble-free, the accuracy was fine; and the rubber feet even kept the bench in place on the workshop floor. There is one machine I have used where I suggested that the manufacturer ought to supply a pair of roller skates to help the user to keep up with the machine! Not so with the Elu.

Wolfcraft Variotech

This is a multi-purpose work bench which can be set up to work as a table saw or as a router table. Made in galvanised steel, it's a really sturdy affair which can be employed in almost any work situation. The table stands 800mm (31½in) high and is 620mm x 565mm (24⅜in by 22¼in) in size. The router, when mounted underneath, is held in safety clamping claws.

The table moves on centre pivots to make for easy access, and is fitted with an angle stop attachment for up to 45° angle cutting; this attachment is, in fact, designed as a sliding and mitre guide with a solid guide bar. A curved milling fence can be mounted through a hole in the bench top. The fence can be used at either side of the cutter, and is held at both ends to give complete stability, while a see-through guard makes for safety. An additional longitudinal-milling stop attachment has its own guard and is so designed for exact parallel guidance, while the milling depth is adjustable. For the production shop where large panels are worked, extensions are available for fitting to one or both sides; these are 610mm (24in) long.

A safety switch can be fitted to the bench leg into which the router can be plugged, giving instant cut-off close to the hand.

122 Elu 551 bench – fitting the router

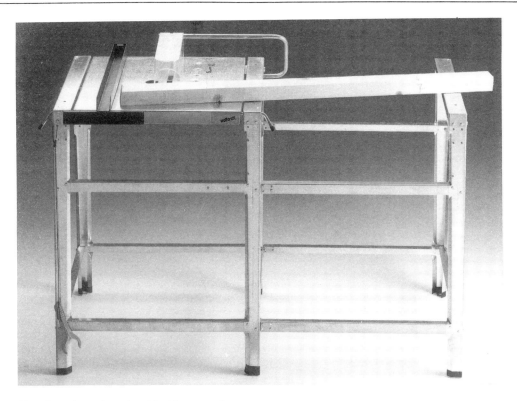

123 Wolfcraft Variotec bench with side extensions

124 Variotec with ball-bearing guide for curved work

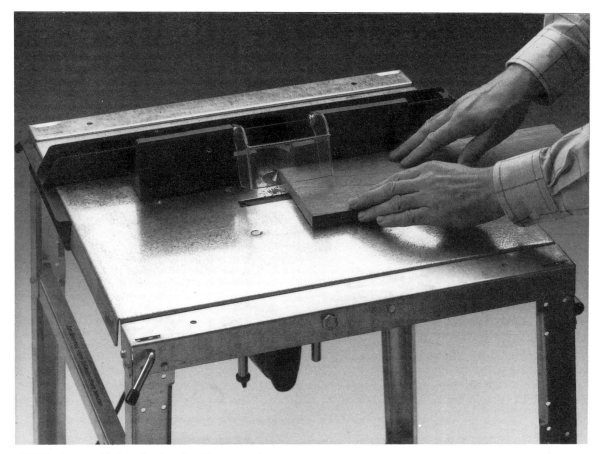

*125 Variotec with longitudinal-milling attachment
in use*

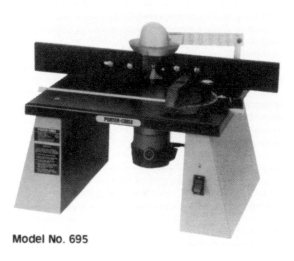

Model No. 695

Porter Cable Company router shaper No695

This is a complete machine, having a table top 457mm by 406mm (18in by 16in), standing 254mm (10in) high. It is fitted with a 1½hp motor running at a no-load speed of 22,000 rpm. Both 6.35mm and 12.7mm (¼in and ½in) shank router cutters can be used. It is fitted with a deep, split fence; and both parts have micro-adjustment. A mitre fence can also be slotted into a groove on the table top. Control is through a 20 amp double-pole switch.

The 696 is exactly the same as the 695, but without the motor and switch. The table is drilled to fit the Porter Cable Co's Nos 514, 518 and 520 routers.

126 Porter Cable Company router shaper No. 695

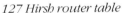

127 Hirsh router table

128 Wolfcraft drill and mill attachment

Hirsh router table

This small router table can be used on top of the normal work bench and there is provision for a permanent bench mounting. The table is 457mm by 330mm (18in by 13in), and stands 280mm (11in) high. The fence is adjustable, and a mitre fence is also fitted. The table is made in rugged structural 'space age' plastic, accurately calibrated and grooved to assist the movement of timber and reduce sawdust build-up. It's an excellent job, particularly for the home craftsman, and it has the advantage of accepting a sabre saw if desired.

Wolfcraft drill and mill attachment

This is another very useful attachment, particularly when the craftsman has in his kit the type of router (such as a Bosch 52) which has a removable motor.

Designed as a drill guide, it is fitted with a Euronorm collar which will receive most drills as well as several routers. The two mounting columns can be set at any angle between 0° and 45°, and the router can be fully plunged. A small router table can be attached to the side of the work bench, and the attachment fixed so that the router becomes a small spindle moulding machine. The attachment can also be fitted with guides for parallel milling and curves.

129 Wolfcraft drill and mill with Hitachi FM8 fitted

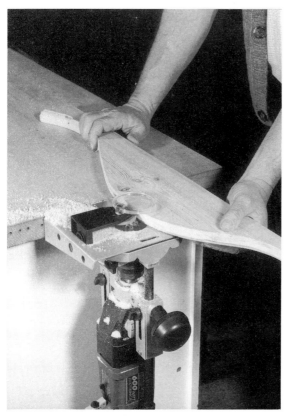

*130 Drill and mill table attached to the side of the
bench – using the guide for cutting curves*

It is most useful for angled work; indeed, there are
few such attachments offering this facility. For the
worker having only limited needs this is probably
the answer.

Router accessories

A drill stand can be a most useful piece of equipment
which, when fitted with a router, will also serve as a
drill or a milling device.

Wolfcraft of West Germany

This manufacturer has several excellent drill stands.
The 4000 Super duty has a 30mm (1³/₁₆in) hexagonal
column which has a height of 550mm (21⅝in); it is·
spring-loaded, and is also fitted with a concertina-
return spring cover. The router is held in position
with wing clamps, and the depth is pre-set. The base

plate measures 220mm by 190mm (8⅝in by 7½in).

The Compass drilling stand also has the hexagonal
column, but the machine head rotates for angle cutting from 0° to 90°. Stroke depth is 60mm (2⅜in).

The 5000 Workshop is a much bigger model, having a base table 370mm by 400mm by 85mm (14½in
by 15¾in by 3⁵/₁₆in) fitted with a round column
50mm (2in) in diameter and 700mm (27½in) high.
The machine head rotates through 0° to 90°, and also
through 360°. A number of accessories can be fitted
to this basic machine; these are shown in action see
page 71.

131 Wolfcraft basic Workshop 5000

Shopsmith router arm

This is a very recent addition to the wide range of equipment available to the router user. Many wood-workers will find the cost of overhead or inverted routing machines too high to justify inclusion in the equipment of a small workshop. The Shopsmith changes all this, as the router arm accommodates any round-bodied router, or one which is designed so that the motor can be withdrawm from the body, like the Hitachi FM8.

The router arm consists of a slotted table, a steel column, a guard and an arm, with a chip-collection chute, all mounted on a sturdy table. A fence, guide

132 Shopsmith router arm

pins and starter pins are also included. The table has a pin-block with interchangeable guide pins; this feature simplifies the making of duplicate parts, and the starter pin will provide more accurate results. Every conceivable cut can be made using this assembly and the accuracy is excellent, as the machine can be checked and adjusted very easily.

The worktable measures 755mm by 451mm (29¾in by 17¾in) and the arm is 755mm (29¾in) long; the overall height is 1.55m (61in).

8 Making Jigs and Fixtures

There are many jigs, fixtures and devices which can be attached to the router to add to its versatility and to simplify the work. Often these are expensive, and buying them can only be justified if they can earn their keep by a reduction in working time, and material wastage. They may also serve to reduce human error.

A number of these devices can be made in the workshop quickly and easily, and the following illustrates some of them. Most have been made from offcuts of plywood, blockboard, particle-board or acrylic sheet, and each and every one is adequate for the task

Housing or dado template

The making of shelf units and bookcases, or any article requiring shelving in its construction, will be simplified with this template. In this case, as with many of the jigs which follow, a guide bush is needed. It is fitted into the base of the router and runs along the edge of any template, be it straight or curved. See page 96 for details.

The reader will be well advised to buy a number of these of different sizes, which, working in conjunction with bits of varying size, will allow the use of one jig to cover a number of different widths of cut.

Hardboard 6mm (¼in) thick is used for the template, and a strip of softwood is employed for the piece which locates against the rear edge of the cabinet or shelf unit uprights. Held in place with a couple of G-cramps, or similar cramps, the template edge checks against location marks on the work to ensure accurate positioning of the housings before cutting. Stopped housings need a stopped slot as in the illustration. The stop is held in place with a panel pin, or double-sided adhesive tape can be used if the slot is open-ended.

Staircase jig

A number of these are available, and for the tradesman the cost of purchase may be justified. Recently, I

133 Template for housing

134 Template for housings stopped at both ends

135 Staircase jig

made a staircase in wych elm and the jig shown was made from 10mm (³⁄₈in) plywood. It proved adequate for the job; the only marking out required on the stringers was a pencil mark for jig location at each tread position, the jig being clamped in place with a G-cramp. The cutter and guide bush were selected before making the jig.

Hinge jigs

Many woodworkers hate hanging doors, perhaps because the principles of hingeing are not clearly understood. With the making of a jig and a clear understanding of the depth the hinge housing has to be sunk, the whole business is simplified. Hinges must be accurately located and the housing cut to a depth equal to the thickness of the hinge leaf. The simple hinge jig shown can be held in place with adhesive tape or hot-melt glue.

Lock jig

We need two jigs for this job; one for sinking the mortise to receive the lock body, and the other to guide the cutting of the recess to house the lock plate. The jig was made to be used for both these cuts, and it can be held in place with double-sided adhesive tape.

136 Hinge and lock jigs

137 Sub-base for boring

Base for boring with the router

The router can be turned into an accurate boring tool, but there is one little difficulty in using the router as it is very hard to centre the bit accurately, since many of the bits have no positive centre which can be used to make an accurate location.

The reader is advised to make a sub-base from acrylic sheet. This must be accurately cut, and a square

shape is best as it can then be used for other purposes. Holes must be drilled and countersunk so that the transparent base can be screwed into place using the screw positions used for the guide bushes. Two lines should then be scribed on the face of the sub-base to locate the centre point accurately; these lines can be darkened with a spot of paint to make sighting easier. Guide lines can be marked on the work piece and the lines on the sub-base lined up with them. When many plunge holes have to be made this device will save a great deal of time and increase accuracy.

Trammel

My first router had no accessories; cash must have been a little thin on the ground! Having to make three radial cuts gave me a problem which I solved by cutting a sub-base, again from acrylic sheet (if you use this material a suitable polish will need to be on hand to keep them in good condition as they scratch easily). Holes were drilled and countersunk in the sub-base so that they could locate on the base of the router; they were accurately marked on a centre line drawn the full length of the sub-base, and drilled at

10mm (⅜in) centres along it. These holes, accurately spaced at precise measurements from the router bit centre point, and used in conjunction with a small locating pin, gave very easy cutting. Indeed, in later years when I actually had a proprietary trammel bar and tried it out, I returned to using the plastic one quite convinced of its simplicity and ease of use.

Fence for corner rebating

Where windows have to be modernised by the insertion of double- or treble-glazed panels, the router can be used to clean out and deepen the existing rebates to receive the thicker glass. Unfortunately, it is impossible to get into the corners of the rebate with the normal fence in position on the router. The addition of an angled fence solves the problem, as it allows the router cutter to work right into the corner. In some cases a long-reach cutter may have to be used, and several progressive cuts taken, in order to avoid overloading both the cutter and the machine. The additional angled fence fits on to the normal router fence, and at the same time a block in front of the fence adds support to the router.

138 Trammel ready for action

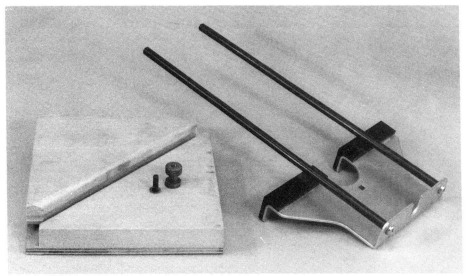

139 Added-on fence for corner rebates

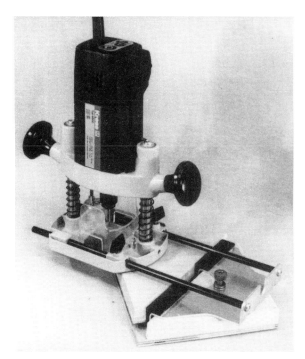

140 Add-on ready for action

Box with hinged template

With repetitive work the need to save time and to make accurate repeats is best served if the work piece is held within a box-type arrangement fitted with a hinged lid which acts as the template. The one in the photograph takes timber up to 38mm (1½in) thick; packing strips of thin wood are used to raise thinner pieces to the correct height for working. This one was made for the routing of the fence panels detailed on page 187. The lid has special hinges which allow the template to be removed and another different design substituted. There are a number of types of lift-off hinges which can be used; alternatively, use those with a removable hinge pin.

141 Box with hinged template

142 Simple jigs

Simple jigs

Many simple jigs can be made using thick plywood or hardboard. The shape should be accurately cut either with the router or a jigsaw, although the router will be found to be much more accurate, and the finish of the edges will be superior. The edges should nevertheless be cleaned up with abrasive paper and wax polish applied to ease the movement of the guide bush. This type of jig can be held down with double-sided adhesive tape or hot-melt glue, but remember to dust the surfaces before applying either to ensure a good grip.

When using this type of jig, move the router as quickly as possible around the curve to avoid any possibility of burning: should any such burning occur it may be necessary to remove a light skim afterwards, but watch that it does not affect the measurements of the work piece.

Additional bases for the router

Sub-bases are useful additions to the router kit, and they will be found at their best when working on large surfaces. The device shown will greatly assist in holding the router steady on long edges when routing grooves or making similar cuts. It helps in getting the router off to a firm start, keeping level and true. It also gives that little added support at the completion of the cut when one is running out of timber. If it is fitted with handles like a plane, these will also help in pushing the router during heavy cutting. The base

143 Large sub-base

can be cut from good-quality plastic sheet at least 6mm (¼in) thick and plane handles can be bought in any good tool store. Alternatively, they could be made on the bench using the router or a jigsaw followed by a spokeshave. It must be remembered that the router's cutting depth is reduced by the thickness of this type of sub-base.

Another useful addition is the base which slides on to the fence arms. This has a handle attached to

144 Added-on handle for greater control

the base which, together with one of the router knobs, provides a grip for the left hand. The base shown is made from a block of beech, bored to receive the fence arms and fixed in position by screws inserted into two threaded bushes let into the block.

Tee-square guide

Another handy addition to the router workshop equipment. Made from a close grained hardwood, it can be cramped in any position on a work piece and its edge used as a guide for routing most types of housings. The tee-squares can be made with the blades at various angles to suit different jobs. I screw and glue the stock and blade together.

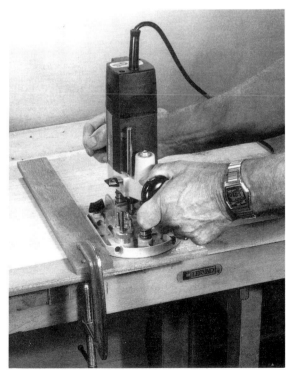

145 Tee-square routing jig

146 Routing guide in use, using the straight edge of the router

147 Eccentric cams used to hold round blank

148 Eccentric cams and stops used to hold round blank

149 Outboard support for the router

Eccentric cams

I first used this idea on a bench hook which I made for handicapped children who had difficulty in holding strips of timber for sawing. There are many applications, and I have seen similar cams used on one of the Sears-Roebuck benches. Mine are made from scraps of particle board faced with plastic laminate. They are bored with the hole offset, and the tail allows the craftsman to rotate the cam to hold work against an upstand or buttons fixed to a piece of scrap board.

The illustration shows a board which can be fixed in the vice; it has upstands at the top and to the left, against which work pieces can be held for routing. I use this one particularly for holding blocks which are to be mounted on the lathe using the expanding collet chuck.

Router support

This consists of a length of timber drilled to receive the fence arms with exactly the same measurements centre-to-centre. In use it provides an extension to the router base and has an outboard knob for added control. I polish the underside to make movement easier.

Useful gauges

Making a number of depth gauges to check the depth of cut of the router cutters is well worthwhile. They will be especially useful when the machine is in-

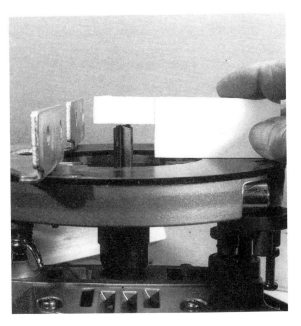

151 Using the depth gauge

verted in a work table or bench to convert it into a spindle moulder, as the normal setting indications cannot easily be seen with the router in this position. Depth gauges will also be found invaluable to check the projection of the cutter with the router on the bench top. They are best made in stout Perspex.

Guide bush gauge

After a little while the value of the number of additions to the equipment for the router will be seen by the purchase of additional guide bushes. To check these using callipers may not only be time-wasting, but also is not really necessary if a block is made into which each one fits accurately. Alternatively, if this is not possible, a gauge strip made with recesses cut exactly to size into which the guides may be tested is a good idea.

Router cutter-shank gauge

Made in Perspex, the top row of holes has the normal shank sizes, while the lower row has cutter diameter sizes. This is much quicker to use than a pair of callipers or a rule.

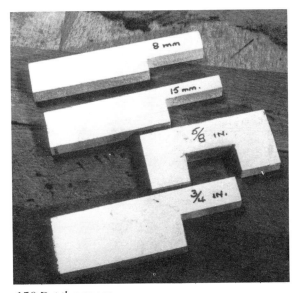

150 Depth gauges

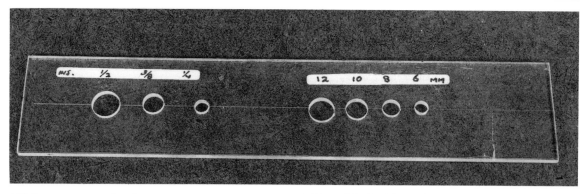

152 Router cutter-shank gauge

153 Adjustable holding frame

154 Adjustable holding frame in use

Adjustable holding frame

These frames are practically indispensable and great time savers. They are made up from slats of multi-plywood which have been slotted by means of the router, this can of course be done on the workbench. They are held together with coach bolts, washers and wing-nuts. If twelve pairs of different lengths are cut, this will give a fair number of options of size. Each frame requires washers cut from the same thickness of plywood to place between the upper and lower slats so that the cramping slats will not be cut with the router when it is passed across the work.

The frame can be set up for square or angle cutting across a board, the top slats acting as a guide for the router which is operated without its fence.

9 Commercial Jigs for the Router

The Leigh dovetail jig

The dovetail joint has long been accepted as the traditional joint used by the cabinet maker, and it requires a high degree of skill in the making. There are several variations of the joint, and it can be used to solve a number of constructional problems in woodwork. Not only is the joint extremely strong, but it can also provide a very attractive feature on a design.

Some workers dismiss the joint as too difficult, and many craftsmen have looked at some of the jigs designed to make the job easier and have dismissed them because they have little scope for the choice of size, or the style of joint.

The Leigh dovetail jig counters all these objections as it offers a very wide range of styles and sizes of dovetailed joints. It has adjustable guide fingers which can be set by measuring with a rule, or by eye. Once set, they can be used to cut both pins and soc-

kets without further alteration, as the finger assembly can be flipped over to present the setting for the members of the joint opposite. In operation it is possible to fine-set the cutting to ensure a perfect fit, indeed, few craftsmen could improve the results.

It is also possible to use the jig for setting up and cutting plain housings or channels (dados in the USA), dovetailed housings, and rebates. The cramping table can also be used to hold work pieces for template routing.

The jig consists of a main frame to which is attached two cramping bars for holding the work piece; the front one holds the job in the vertical position, and the rear one holds it in the horizontal. A finger assembly is contained in the body of the frame, mounted on two sliding brackets which can be adjusted with finger assembly scales calibrated to ensure accuracy.

The finger assembly itself comprises a series of in-

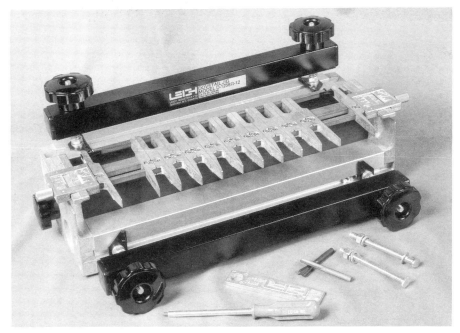

155 Leigh dovetail jig

finitely adjustable fingers with left and right hand sides, and they slide upon a large and small pair of rails. The router, fitted with a guide bush, runs against this assembly when cutting the dovetail pins and sockets. Spacing between the fingers can be varied and set using 'square-drive' screws which have square sockets (a Canadian invention and an exceedingly good one, but not seen in screwdrivers in the UK or USA). A cross-cut bar can be fitted into the rounded finger ends, and this is used when straight-cutting sliding dovetails, lapped dovetails (called half-blind in the USA), rebates and grooves.

The jig is supplied with a special 8° angled dovetail cutter of the tungsten-carbide type. This gives the deepest and most narrow cut possible and the slope strikes a happy medium between that suggested for softwoods (1 in 6) and hardwoods (1 in 8). The manufacturers also provide straight cutters for cutting the pins, and also offer other sizes to suit particular needs, plus two sizes of jig 305mm and 610mm (12in and 24in) to cover almost every job size, and spare fingers.

Both side stops and angled side stops can be fitted to the jig to ensure correct alignment of the work pieces with each other. The two parts of the joint are cut separately, the finger assembly being flipped over to change from the angled finger ends to the straight ones. When the jig is used in a production set-up, the use of two routers would cut down both the setting-up and the cutting time, one router being used for the sockets and the other for the tails.

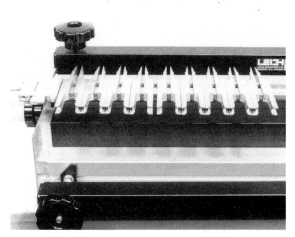

156 Leigh dovetail jig showing fingers

158 Leigh dovetail jig fingers flipped over

157 Leigh dovetail jig fingers and size setting

159 Making adjustments – pins – fingers flipped over and cutter size being set

The Keller jig

This is made in California and is probably the most straightforward jig obtainable for cutting dovetails.

The jig consists of two well-machined templates made in aluminium, one template being for the pins, and the other for the sockets. Most jigs have a limited capacity which rarely extends beyond 610mm (24in); since this one doesn't include in its design a means of holding the timber, if a very large piece is being worked on the jig can be re-positioned along its length.

160 Keller jig with bits having ball-bearing guides

There are three models. Model 1600 has templates 407mm (16in) long, with a timber thickness capacity of 5mm to 16mm (³⁄₈in to ⁵⁄₈in). Model 2400 has templates 610mm (24in) long, with a timber capacity of 10mm to 25mm (³⁄₈in to 1in); while the templates of the 3600 are 915mm (36in) long, and the model accepts timber 16mm to 32mm (⁵⁄₈in to 1¼in) thick. Each of the jigs comes complete with ball-bearing guided router cutters with shank sizes of 6.35mm (¼in) for the 1600, and 12.7mm (½in) for the other two models. This makes for easy setting-up and eliminates the need for guide bushes.

The following table shows the angle of the pins, the major width, and the centre-to-centre pin spacing, and these factors determine the pattern of the dovetail joint.

The smaller capacity jig is ideal for small cabinets, drawer making and boxes, but the mid-size model 2400 would be best for the serious home craftsman and the small production workshop. Although the templates have fixed spacings, they can be moved along the work to vary the positions of the dovetails and thus provide very attractive jointing. Obviously this takes up a little time and requires greater care, but where time is not vital it's a decorative feature.

Joint pattern	1600	2400	3600
Pins: angle of cut x major width	7° x 11mm (⁷⁄₁₆in)	7° x 16mm (⁵⁄₈in)	14° x 25mm (1in)
Pin spacing: centre-to-centre	29mm (1⅛in)	45mm (1¾in)	76mm (3in)

Vermont American

These people make the smallest capacity jig I have ever seen, 203mm (8in). Obviously, this very limited capacity seriously affects the usefulness of the tool, yet many woodworkers undertake small work, and the jig is a fine one – not to be ignored! The actual template itself is double-sided to produce 6mm and 12mm (¼in and ½in) dovetails. A fine adjustment device is fitted at each end of the machine, and the whole job is well made.

Shapercraft dovetailer

This is a small jig which has been designed for use with either a power drill or a router. It comprises an angled cutter guide and an angled cutter holder which slides in slots in the guide. The holder can be fitted with a dovetail cutter for dovetailing and a straight cutter for comb jointing. The jig accepts timber up to 152mm (6in) wide and 19mm (³⁄₄in) thick, but with care any width of timber can be jointed by moving the frame across. Suitable cramps are required. Calibrations in metric are built-in, and depth setting is controlled with a depth collar screwed on to the holder. Very little marking out is needed apart from face marks or numbers indicating the inner or outer faces of the job.

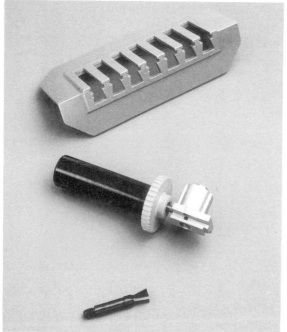

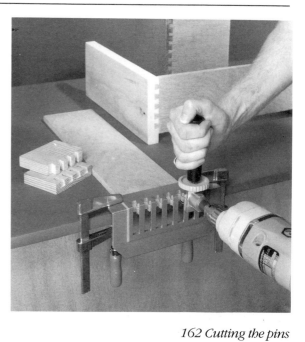

161 Shapercraft dovetail 6000A

162 Cutting the pins

163 Cutting the sockets

Elu dovetailing jig

A very well made jig which enables 12mm (½in) dovetails to be cut in timber between 12mm and 20mm (½in and ¹³/₁₆in) thick and up to 300mm (11¾in) wide.

It consists of a plate with straight fingers which can be attached and adjusted on a main frame, which in turn is screwed to a board. The main frame has top and side clamps for holding both components of the joint, which is cut at one setting. It is recommended that the router is fitted with a fine-depth adjuster and a trial joint made to ensure a close fit.

An excellent addition to the kit is a depth-setting gauge for the cutter which, when used in conjunction with the fine-depth adjuster, ensures complete accuracy.

164 Elu dovetailing jig

Sears-Roebuck dovetailing jig

This jig has several novel features; for example the templates are double-sided for making both 6mm and 12mm (¼in and ½in) dovetails, and a double-sided template can also be bought to simplify the making of box-comb joints. The work can be safely held, and although the base is of plastic it seems to be adequate.

Porter Cable Company dovetailing jig

This is a sturdy jig, well-made and fitted with an excellent means of accurate adjustment by using an Allen key.

Bosch dovetailing jig

Very well made, this jig is extremely strong; the base is made of extruded aluminium and is in marked contrast to a number of others. Its clamping system holds the work very firmly, and thank goodness for the better quality and design of tightening knob! A novel feature which helps to keep the work in place is the milling on the base piece. Two models give 305mm and 407mm (12in and 16in) timber capacity respectively, and can accept a timber thickness of 25mm (1in).

Sears-Roebuck

This very large company has the widest range of accessories for the router, and they are available both in the UK and the USA. A close examination of them by both serious amateur woodworkers and professional craftsmen will prove well worthwhile. Unlike many router accessories, these are inexpensive and seem well made.

The drawer and panel decorator

This consists of an extruded aluminium frame which can be clamped around a panel and used as a guide for the router. It is extremely accurate and can accommodate panels of up to 863mm (34in) square. Seven corner templates are supplied, and others could be made and fitted to a blank template holder which is also provided. Curves can also be scribed with the panel. Three templates are supplied for cutting fielded panels and many variations of these can be cut in 3mm (⅛in) hardboard. The device will save its cost in one batch of kitchen cupboard doors.

165 Sears drawer and panel decorator with corner templates fitted

Letter and numeral template kits
This kit enables letters and numbers to be cut in 35mm and 63mm (1½in and 2½in) sizes, and it can be used with all routers. The templates can be set in a clamp; there are nine numerals, 26 letter and 5 punctuation marks. The kit requires a set of guide bushes.

Rout-a-Sign
This is an extension of the lettering set, and letters and numerals can be routed from 19mm to 115mm (¾in to 4½in) high. The router is assembled on steel bars and works from a template fixed to the work-frame. The latter accepts boards of any length and between 51mm and 254mm (2in and 10in) in width; the thickness must be between 12mm and 51mm (½in and 2in). A carousel which carries all the templates is attached; it should be noted that the letters and numerals are italic and slope to the right. A router with a circular base is needed, but sub-bases are offered by most router manufacturers, or one could be made up in the workshop.

For the woodworker who wishes to offer a service in signs this could well be the answer, and it should not be beyond the skills of most craftsmen to add to the number of templates and so make for greater variety.

Router Lathe or Router-Crafter
I have a device which fits to my lathe which I designed for fluting table legs. This uses my Kress router and makes an excellent job of parallel and tapered flutes of various sections. I use the Multi-star chuck, which can also be used as a dividing head.

The Sears Router Lathe makes straight and tapered turned parts with beads, coves, and flutes both around and lengthwise on legs of every sort, and also on lamp stands and similar work. It will also execute contour turnings following a pre-cut pattern, as well as left and right hand spirals. The number of different combinations of pattern is infinite.

The equipment consists of a sturdy diecast aluminium framework and chromium-plated metal tubes, and the router is mounted in clamps. Most routers will fit, and the Crafter will accept timber between 25mm and 76mm (1in and 3in) square or round, 915mm (36in) long.

This can be a fun machine, as well as a useful addition to the workshop for making those odd jobs which could normally be very time-consuming.

Edgecrafter

This is another clever accessory but it has to be attached to the router table. The tool comprises a base and overarm assembly, and if you are using another style of table, some adjustments will have to be made to fit it. The base is fitted instead of the normal straight fence. There are four templates supplied, and others could quickly be made in hardboard.

The guide and template are centred on the table or stool top work piece and placed on overarm assembly. The template roller guide will follow the contour of the template when the work piece is rotated against the router bit. Edges can be routed to any number of different combinations of template and router bit shapes on work pieces up to 30 inches in diameter. If pieces larger than 36 inches are assembled, the adjustable support bracket assists in supporting it.

To summarise, there are three basic operations:

1. Rounding of both inside and outside edges.
2. Making beads, coves, and steps, around both inside and outside edges.
3. Shaping the inside and outside edges using templates. By using more than one router bit a wide variety of shapes can be achieved.

Four templates are supplied and others can easily be made.

Router-Recreator

The purist wood carver will not be rushing out to buy one, but if copies must be made of a small carving this is the accessory to use. It can be used to make three-dimensional figures and a number of other pieces up to 203mm by 203mm (8in by 8in).

Router pantograph

Can be used to carve three-dimensional figures and to make dimensional drawings. It also reproduces forms, line drawings, letters, numerals, and 40°, 50° and 60° reductions. Letters and numerals can be 90mm, 115mm and 140mm (3½in, 4½in, and 5½in) high in upper and lower case, and in Old English, Oriental, Script, Modern and Computer (uppercase only) styles.

Two-dimensional router pantograph

This is similar to the three-dimensional one, and makes line drawings, Modern style upper and lower case letters and numerals in 42°, 50° and 58° reductions.

Multi-purpose edge guide

This is a useful addition to the router kit as it combines the functions of a laminate trimmer, edge guide and trammel point. It can only be used on a router with a circular base.

Wolfcraft dovetailer and comb-jointer

This is a small unit which I bought many years ago. It can accept up to 152mm (6in) wide stock, but it can be used on wider material by careful re-setting. The making of boxes using either dovetailed or comb-jointed is simplified; and although adjustments on the jig itself are not possible, the resulting joints fit well. The router cutters are 'specials' – being screwed into the chuck – and are supplied with the machine. Timber up to a thickness of 25mm (1in) can be worked. Although the attachment was designed for use with a power drill, it can also be used with those routers which have removable bodies.

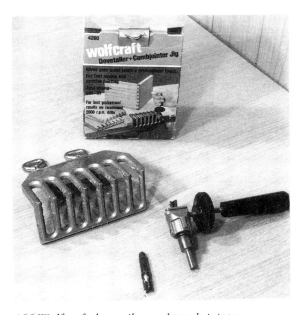

166 Wolfcraft dovetailer and comb-jointer

167 Staircase jig for traditional tread and riser work *168 Staircase jig – open-tread version*

Trend staircase routing jig

The professional user will find that this jig will pay for its cost with the first staircase. It's a simple, hard plastic plate which will not distort, and this is fitted with a reversible fence and clamp to give exact matching of the staircase strings. It can be adjusted to suit varying widths of strings and any heavy-duty router can be used. For this work it is recommended that a wide, larger sub-base is fitted to add greater stability and to ease the movement of the router over the jig.

There is a separate version of the jig for open-tread stairs (Fig 168).

10 Routing with Templates

The use of templates greatly expands the range of work possible with a router, while the simple addition of a central guide bush fitted to the underside of the base to act as a fence eliminates the use of the standard fences and guide pins. The guide bush itself acts as the fence, and being of small radius, permits the movement of the bit around really small curves, since guide bushes are available as small as 10mm diameter.

Many repetitive jobs can be time-consuming as well as boring. When this type of work has to be done, the making of a once-and-for-all template (or pattern, if you wish) will ensure consistent accuracy and cut down the time taken. Templates can be stored against future use, and if they are made in durable material will give a lifetime of service. Hardboard, plywood, Tufnol plastic or metal sheets can all be used. Do not use timber unless it is completely stable, as warping and distortion can seriously affect the path of the cutter. The thickness of the material used will be dictated by the depth of the guide bush – it must obviously be slightly more than

the guide bush in order to clear the face of the work and allow easy passage of the router.

Templates for standard jobs such as housings for shelving, hinge recesses (known as 'gains' in the USA), and lock recesses should be a part of the workshop equipment. Some of these are shown in Chapter 10.

Manufacturers have made a number of contributions to this field. Some of the dovetailing jigs are described in Chapter 9 and are also used in the project section of this book.

Patterns can be cut using the router freehand, or by means of the jigsaw or the bandsaw. The cutting should be as fine and clean as possible, and I usually treat the edges with wax polish to improve the movement of the guide pin or bush. Alternatively, the bowsaw or the coping saw could be used, but it is suggested that as far as possible the router itself be used – its versatility is unsurpassed.

Unfortunately, most router manufacturers fail to appreciate the need for a variety of sizes of guides, but it is at least fortunate that for the most part the distance between the fixing screw holes in the bases of many routers is the same. Trend Machinery & Cutting Tools Ltd make a complete range of guide bushes from 10mm to 40mm (3/8in to 1 9/16in) outside diameter; they can also be bought in sets.

The guide bush should be selected to allow the cutter just to pass through, as this will permit the router to follow the template closely. It must be remembered that with large guides close detail is impossible.

Templates can be internal and external. Many woodworkers doing repetitive work make dummy boxes with hinged lids, the latter being the template and the box serving to locate the work piece and hold it firmly. A number of methods of holding templates is shown in Chapter 12. Setting up and using the template soon becomes a simple matter, and the number of applications is infinite.

169 Various styles of guide bushes

CUTTER DIAMETERS IN INCHES	CUTTER DIAMETERS IN MM	GUIDE BUSH SIZE – OUTSIDE DIAM. IN MILLIMETRES														
		10	12	14	16	17	18	20	22	24	26	27	28	30	32	40
7/64	3.0	3.5	4.5	5.5	6.5	7.0	7.5	8.5	9.5	10.5	11.5	12.0	12.5	13.5	14.5	18.5
1/8	3.2	3.4	4.4	5.4	6.4	6.9	7.4	8.4	9.4	10.4	11.4	11.9	12.4	13.4	14.4	18.4
5/32	4	3.0	4.0	5.0	6.0	6.5	7.0	8.0	9.0	10.0	11.0	11.5	12.0	13.0	14.0	18.0
3/16	4.8	2.6	3.6	4.6	5.6	6.1	6.6	7.6	8.6	9.6	10.6	11.1	11.6	12.6	13.6	17.6
13/64	5.0	2.5	3.5	4.5	5.5	6.0	6.5	7.5	8.5	9.5	10.5	11.0	11.5	12.5	13.5	17.5
7/32	5.5	2.2	3.2	4.2	5.2	5.7	6.2	7.2	8.2	9.2	10.2	10.7	11.2	12.2	13.2	17.2
15/64	6.0	2.0	3.0	4.0	5.0	5.5	6.0	7.0	8.0	9.0	10.0	10.5	11.0	12.0	13.0	17.0
1/4	6.3	1.8	2.8	3.8	4.8	5.3	5.8	6.8	7.8	8.8	9.8	10.3	10.8	11.8	12.8	16.8
5/16	8.0	1.0	2.0	3.0	4.0	4.5	5.0	6.0	7.0	8.0	9.0	9.5	10.0	11.0	12.0	16.0
23/64	9.0	X	1.5	2.5	3.5	4.0	4.5	5.5	6.5	7.5	8.5	9.0	9.5	10.5	11.5	15.5
3/8	9.5	X	1.2	2.2	3.2	3.7	4.2	5.2	6.2	7.2	8.2	8.7	9.2	10.2	11.2	15.2
25/64	10.0	X	1.0	2.0	3.0	3.5	4.0	5.0	6.0	7.0	8.0	8.5	9.0	10.0	11.0	15.0
7/16	11.0	X	X	1.5	2.5	3.0	3.5	4.5	5.5	6.5	7.5	8.0	8.5	9.5	10.5	14.5
15/32	12.0	X	X	1.0	2.0	2.5	3.0	4.0	5.0	6.0	7.0	7.5	8.0	9.0	10.0	14.0
1/2	12.7	X	X	X	1.6	2.1	2.6	3.6	4.6	5.6	6.6	7.1	7.6	8.6	9.6	13.6
	13.0	X	X	X	1.5	2.0	2.5	3.5	4.5	5.5	6.5	7.0	7.5	8.5	9.5	13.5
	15.0	X	X	X	X	1.0	1.5	2.5	3.5	4.5	5.5	6.0	6.5	7.5	8.5	12.5
5/8	16.0	X	X	X	X	X	X	2.0	3.0	4.0	5.0	5.5	6.0	7.0	8.0	12.0
	18.0	X	X	X	X	X	X	1.0	2.0	3.0	4.0	4.5	5.0	6.0	7.0	11.0
23/32	18.2	X	X	X	X	X	X	X	1.9	2.9	3.9	4.4	4.9	5.9	6.9	10.9
3/4	19.00	X	X	X	X	X	X	X	1.5	2.5	3.5	4.0	4.5	5.5	6.5	10.5
	20.00	X	X	X	X	X	X	X	1.0	2.0	3.0	3.5	4.0	5.0	6.0	10.0
7/8	22.2	X	X	X	X	X	X	X	X	1.9	2.9	2.4	3.9	4.9	5.9	8.9
1	25.5	X	X	X	X	X	X	X	X	X	X	0.7	1.2	2.2	3.2	7.2
1 1/8	28.5	X	X	X	X	X	X	X	X	X	X	X	X	X	1.7	5.7

Guide bush selection

When templates are in use, precise details of the relationship between the guide bush and the cutter are needed.

The drawings show the relationship between the template and the guide bush for both inside and outside profile work. The shaded area shows the size-difference between the cutter and the outside diameter of the guide bush.

A number of routers have no provision for the fitting of guide bushes, and some have bushes which are larger than the standard bushes shown in Fig 171. Fortunately, a circular base plate can be obtained and fitted to the router to overcome this problem. My Elu 177E is one such machine.

When fitted, this base plate will receive the standard size guide bushes which are seen in the Trend list in fifteen sizes from 10mm to 40mm (3⁄8in to 19⁄16in) outside diameter.

172 Elu 177E with sub-base to accept standard bushes

171 Fitting a guide bush to the Elu 177E

173 Round sub-base fitted and standard guide bush screwed in place

174 Circular base plate with guide bushes

175 Fitting the circular sub-base

Procedure for template work

1 Sketch out the design on paper.
2 Choose the cutter best suited by size and style to carry out the work.
3 Select a guide bush which will allow the cutter to pass through without any possibility of its touching the side as this would ruin both the guide bush and the cutter.
4 Measure the outside diameter of the guide bush and subtract the diameter of the cutter from it. Divide this figure by two to give the amount by which the template will be larger or smaller than the finished job, depending on whether it is an inside or outside template.

Remember to check the depth of the guide bush, and choose the thickness of material for the template that will give clearance – otherwise the guide will be running on the template and also on the work.

The template can now be set out accurately on the selected material. Transferring the design from the paper can easily be effected by using carbon-paper if the material being used is hardboard or plywood; should plastic or metal have been chosen, the drawing should be glued to it.

After cutting, clean up the edges if necessary to ensure an easy passage for the guide bush. Polish the edges with a good wax polish or paraffin wax. If plywood or hardboard have been used for the template, clean up the faces as well, and add a touch of polish to them. Plastic sheet may also need a little cleaning up and polishing – do this with the proprietary brand of polish suggested by the makers of the material; however, metal cleaning polish, which has a slightly abrasive quality, will do fine.

Marking up for template making and for freehand routing

For accurate work, a preliminary drawing is essential. Transferring the drawing to the work piece can be done in a number of ways apart from using carbon paper. A half-pattern can be made for the curve of a table rail, for instance, by drawing one half, folding the paper at the halfway point, and then cutting along the line with scissors. Opening out the sheet will give a perfectly symmetrical curve which can then be glued or pasted to the work piece.

For a table top, one quarter of the curve is drawn with the paper already folded into quarters. Cut and

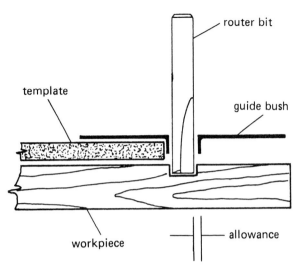

176 Working out the allowance

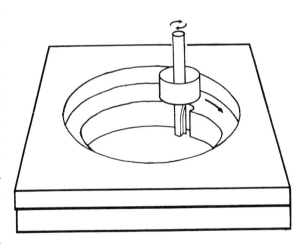

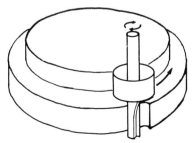

177 Using the templates – inside template
– outside template

opened out, this will give a perfect guide which can be pasted on or marked around with a pencil.

If a copy has to be made of a drawing, the best method is to mark up the drawing in small squares. Take a piece of graph paper, draw up the size to which the new drawing has to be made, and plot the points from the the master to the graph paper. If the original drawing has to be preserved, place a piece of transparent paper over it and mark the grid on that so that the original is unmarked. If a drawing has to be enlarged, the best method is to mark over it with a grid of small squares of a convenient size, such as 12mm (½in) or 25mm (1in), drawing it in on an overlay if necessary. Then, on a larger piece of paper, draw an identical grid but with the squares made bigger by the amount of the enlargement required. Thus if the grid is composed of 12mm (½in) squares and the larger grid squares are 25mm (1in) the enlarged drawing will be doubled in size (ignoring the small discrepancies in size between metric and Imperial dimensions). The same procedure can be carried out in reverse to reduce a drawing.

Plain teak stand and teak stand with tiled insert

11 Selecting Router Cutters

As with all woodworking tools, great care should be taken in the selection of the right ones for the job. This particularly applies to router cutters, since they have to work at very high speeds and in many cases are of quite complex shapes. In addition, they must work in a great variety of hard and softwoods, and at the same time produce a perfect surface, this being one which should not demand the use of different grades of abrasive paper. Router cutters are expensive, and work much harder than any other woodworking cutting edge; therefore, they must be made with considerable expertise and the precise knowledge of the jobs they have to do.

An incorrectly chosen cutter can break down in seconds; indeed, its edge can be ripped away when cutting some materials for which it is not suitable. A good example is the HSS (high-speed steel) cutter when it is used on particle board; this material has timber chips of varying hardness and quality in its composition, plus a very hard glue, and often a considerable quantity of grit. These, in combination, serve to destroy the edge in seconds – a cutter made of material designed for the job must be chosen. For most timbers high-speed steel provides a superb edge, and if the woodworker generally employs this material using the bits infrequently, then it will be found adequate.

Cutters for man-made timbers like particle board, blockboard, plywood, and medium-density fibre board (MDF), must be tungsten-carbide tipped (TCT). With the growth of man-made boards after 1945, it became obvious that materials used in the making of tools, bits, and cutters would have to undergo considerable changes and the tungsten-carbide tipped tool was born. Tungsten carbide is a very hard but nevertheless brittle material; tiny pieces are brazed to tool-steel stock and provide an

edge which will last some thirty times longer than high speed steel. The edges can be sharpened but need special treatment, and the tips can be replaced when worn.

Cutters are also available in solid tungsten; they are usually in the smaller sizes and are generally bought for special jobs. It is possible to buy tungsten-carbide tips of thinner section which can be discarded after they have been sharpened a number of times. Even harder materials have to be used for many jobs, and probably the ultimate is the diamond-tipped cutter. Here we find diamond crystals bonded to carbide to form an extremely sharp and long-lasting edge, but the cost is high by comparison with TCT cutters. Special cutters are also available for cutting re-inforced glass fibre; these look rather like rasps as they have similar teeth.

Cutters (or bits as they are referred to in the USA) are available in hundreds of different shapes and sizes as well as in several different styles. The most common are those which can either be used in the router working in freehand style, or with the addition of a fence fitted either to the router itself, or with the router attached to a router table fitted with its own fence. This type of cutter can be used to make straightforward cuts such as rebates and grooves, and also to form a very large variety of decorative edges and to assist in the cutting of some joints.

Straight cutters. Sometimes called 'panel cutters' are produced with single or double flutes, the latter giving the best cut. Those with two flutes can be obtained with or without bottom-cutting edges. Fig 178A shows the single flute cutter; and Fig 178B the two flute.

Vee-groove cutters. These can be used for a variety of decorative work; Fig 178C.

Cove or radius cutter. A very useful cutter made in many sizes which can be used for decorative work as well as cutting drip grooves in window and door frames. They can also be employed in the cutting of

Carved number plate and incised lettering

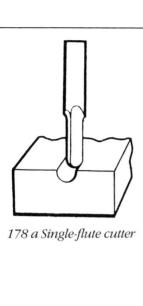

178 a Single-flute cutter

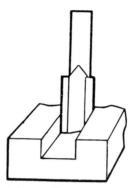

b Two-flute cutter

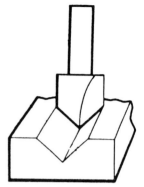

c Vee-groove cutter

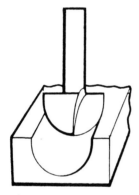

d Core or radius cutter

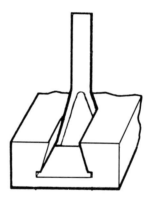

e Dovetail cutter

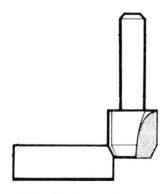

179 a Laminate trimmer

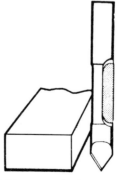

b Pierce-and-trim cutter

c Slitter and shank cutter

trays, removal of the groundwork in wood carving, and other work; Fig 178D.

Dovetail cutter. For use with dovetailing jigs in the cutting of through and lapped dovetails; also for cutting dovetailed housings (dados in the USA). Shown in Fig 178E.

Laminate trimmer. An essential tool where plastic laminates have to be trimmed; Fig 179A.

Pierce-and-trim cutters. Often cut-outs have to be made and these cutters have been designed to first bore a hole through the material using the specially designed point, and then traversed through the work with the edge doing the cutting; Fig 179B.

Slitter and shank cutters. Used to cut a slot in the edge of a board to fit a plastic or other type lipping; Fig 179C.

Another group of cutters is fitted with small guide pins at the lower ends permitting the router and cutter to work without the addition of a fence. This is ideal for the cutting and shaping of edges, both straight and curved; they can also be used with the router attached to a router table. Many shapes and sizes are available.

Rebate cutters. These can be used for the cutting of rebates and grooves, and for open housings across the grain; also for the cutting of joints and other straight work where the waste wood has to be removed quickly and cleanly; see Fig 180A.

Chamfer cutters. For chamfering and vee-grooving; Fig 180B.

Ovolo cutters. This is the most popular shape in use, and there are many cutters made with variations of the basic shape; Fig 180C.

Rounding-over cutter. Used in a similar way to the chamfer bit and will be found useful in cabinet work as well as in the making of architraves and skirting boards; Fig 180D.

Trimmer cutter. A straightforward trimming cutter used for trimming plastic laminate edges; Fig 180E.

An addition, indeed a refinement of the fixed guide pin, is found in those which are fitted with a self-guide bearing. Some of the cutters are fitted with fixed bearings, others have removable ones. In the latter case, there may well be various sizes of bearings to suit different requirements. This type of cutter can also appear as an arbor, to which can be fitted a variety of shaped cutters and various sizes of self-guide bearings. These are extremely versatile and in

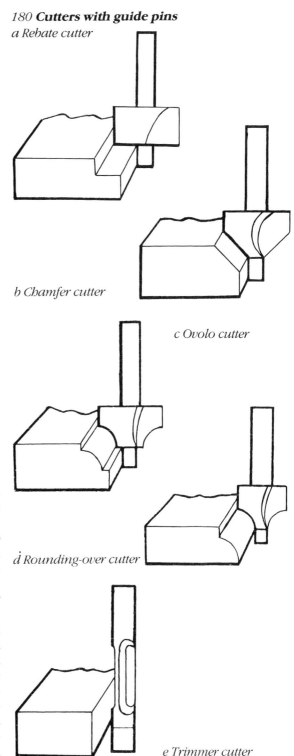

180 **Cutters with guide pins**
a Rebate cutter

b Chamfer cutter

c Ovolo cutter

d Rounding-over cutter

e Trimmer cutter

181 *Cutters with ball-bearing guides*

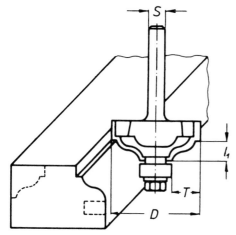

a Roman ogee cutter with fillet

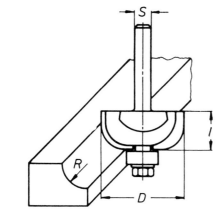

b Cove cutter

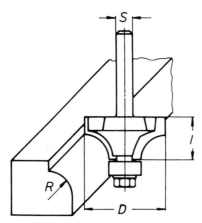

c Rounding-over cutter

production work they have the advantage of cutting costs.

Some shapes are: Roman ogee Fig 181A; Cove cutter Fig 181B; Rounding-over Fig 181C.

Router cutters with interchangeable shanks. This is a recent innovation comprising shanks screwed at one end to receive different cutter heads. Shanks are available to suit any router collet, and a wide range of standard and innovative heads is available.

This is a great cost-cutter and increases the versatility of the workshop. The heads follow the accepted style, being plain, fixed pin or self-guide bearings.

Some of the most popular of these are:

Without guide pin:
Vee-grooving and chamfering; Fig 182A.
Profile cutter, Fig 182B.
Beading cutter Fig 182C.
Core cutter; Fig 182D.

With fixed guide pin:
Chamfer
Rebate
Rounding-over
Profile
Multi-radius

With self-guide bearings:
Beading cutter, useful for quarter-rounds, beading, and rounding over; Fig 183A.
Cove cutter; Fig 183B.
Multi-profile cutter for rounding over quarter-rounds, beading, coving, and profiling. Can be used with or without the guide; Fig 183C.
Profiling cutter with similar uses to the above; Fig 183D.

182 **Cutters with interchangeable shanks**

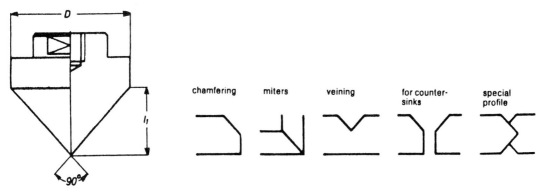

chamfering   miters   veining   for counter-sinks   special profile

a Vee-grooving and chamfer cutter

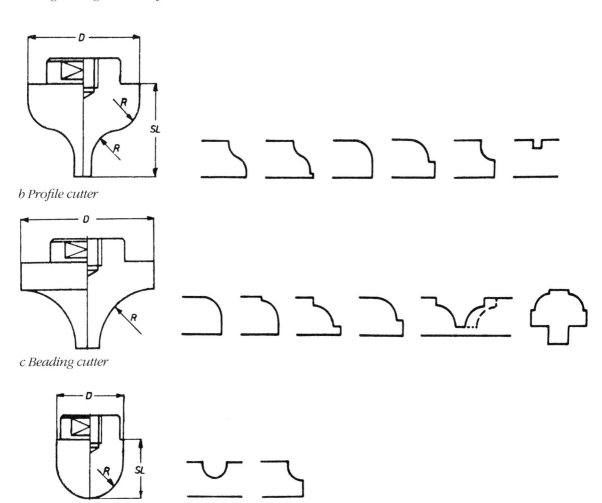

b Profile cutter

c Beading cutter

d Core box cutter

*182   **Cutters with interchangeable shanks
        and solid guide pins***

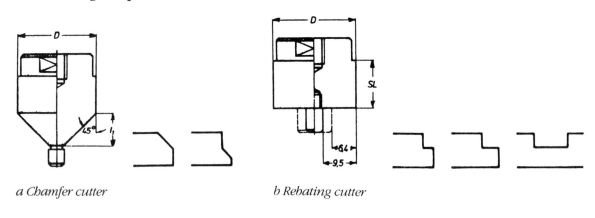

a *Chamfer cutter*   b *Rebating cutter*

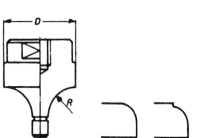

c *Rounding-over cutter*   d *Profile cutter*

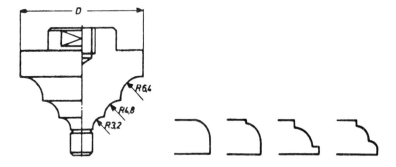

e *Multi-radius cutter*

183 **Cutters with interchangeable shanks and ball-bearing guides**

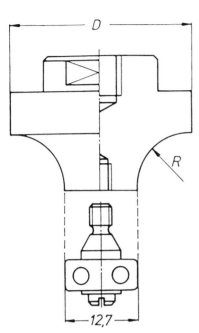

a Beading cutter

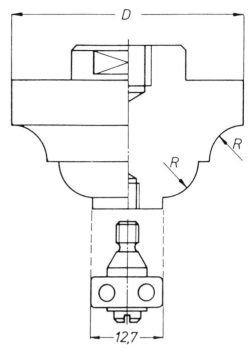

b Cove cutter

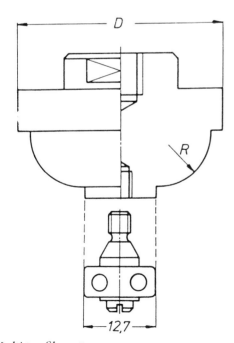

c Multi-profile cutter

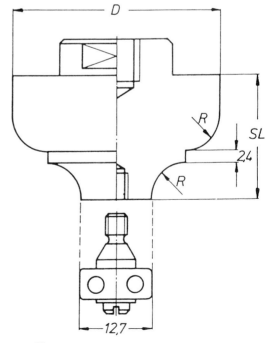

d Profiling cutter

184

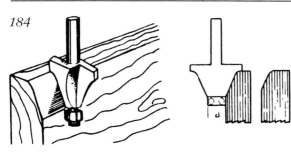

a Rounding-over/chamfer cutter

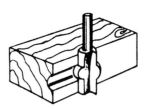

f Staff bead jointer

b Classic-style cutter

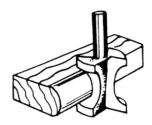

g Staff bead cutter

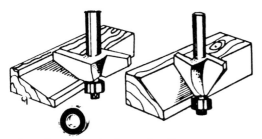

c Chamfer and raised panel cutter

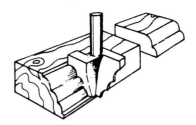

h Multi-mould bead kit

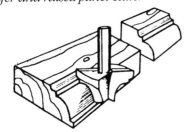

d Classic ovolo

k Pointed round and ogee

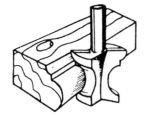

e Classic staff bead

l Sash bar ovolo

A wide choice of special cutters, in a variety of shapes and sizes, can solve most of the problems associated with wood shaping. Many are variations on the traditional patterns, and others are the answers to the trends in modern day machine-production. Typical of these are:

Rounding-over and chamfer cutter for use in the making of skirting boards and architraves. Usually fitted with a self-guide bearing; Fig 184A.

Classic-style cutter. These can be used in fielded-panel work and, in reverse, in drop-leaf table construction; Fig 184B.

Chamfer and raised panel cutter. For many types of moulding and panelling; Fig 184C.

Classic ovolo – probably the best-known shape for table and sideboard edging on period-style furniture; Fig 184D.

Classic staff bead. This is used to give added attractiveness to edgings; Fig 184E.

Staff bead jointer. Used to make excellent tongued joints in long boards; Fig 184F.

Staff bead cutter which can be used to decorate an edge; Fig 184G.

Multimould. This can be used in whole or in part to produce various shapes of mouldings; Fig 184H.

Pointed round and ogee. For decorative grooving, moulding, and beading. Also used for decorative work on turned legs, table lamps, and lampstands; Fig 184K.

Sash bar ovolo. Designed for the cutting of window sash bars, it can also be used for architraves, edges and similar work; Fig 184L.

Fielded-panel sets. These are very popular and are seen in any number of curve-combinations. They are sold as sets; as follows:

Ovolo scriber set – probably the most popular; Fig 185A.

Sashbar ovolo set. Can be used for both sash bar and fielded-panel work; Fig 185B.

Classic panel set. A classic edge moulding with reverse moulding for fielded-panel work; Fig 185C.

185

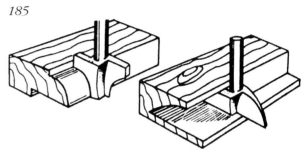

a Ovolo scriber set

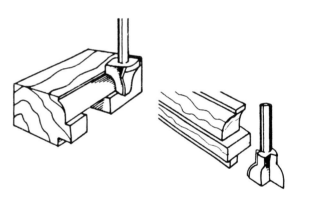

b Sash bar ovolo set

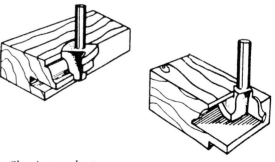

c Classic panel set

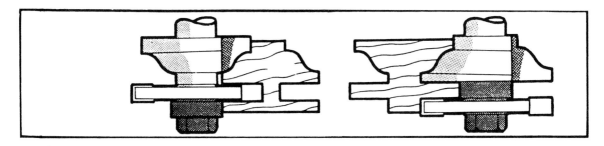

186 Classic profile scriber set

187 Set of classic profile cutters for door-frame construction

An extension of this group is seen in the fielded-panel combination set which is made up of a moulding cutter, a groover, and a self-guide bearing. This cuts a classic mould and groove, and in reverse, a matching shape and tongue.

With the ever-increasing use of plastic laminates on man-made boards, the finishing of these extremely hard materials needs a whole range of special cutters. All must be tungsten-carbide tipped, or made in solid carbide.

90° Trimmer bit. This is used to trim the top edges of plastic laminate. An addition can be made to this type of bit in the form of a slitting blade which cuts a groove in the edge of the material into which can be fitted purpose made plastic edging; Fig 188A.

90° Laminate trimmer. This type of cutter can be used to trim both the vertical faces of a board using the bottom cutting edge, and the overlapping horizontal edge. It can also be used to rebate all man-made boards and similar materials, and also aluminium; Fig 188B.

Bevel trimmers. These are available with 30°, 45°, 60° and 80° angles and are used as an alternative to the 90° variety particularly when a wider edge line is needed; Fig 188C.

Combination laminate trimmer. Covers; lip trimming, top trimming, and bevelling; Fig 188D.

Laminate pierce-and-trim. Designed to pierce and cut out apertures in laminated work-tops, the point of the cutter serves to bore through the board, while the side cuts the profile, and the lower part of the cutter acts as a guide pin; Fig 188E.

Solid carbide cutters. These are ideal for the home craftsman since they are cheaper than the tipped variety. They cover 90° and 60° angle trimming; one of the cutters has a guide pin; Fig 188F.

188 **Laminate trimmers**

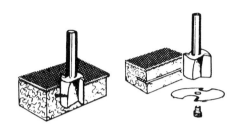

a 90° for top surface work with edge slitter

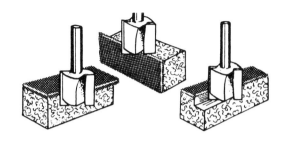

b Other 90° trimmers

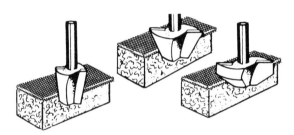

c Bevel trimmer

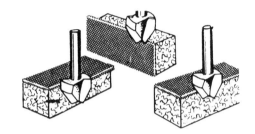

d Combination laminate trimmer

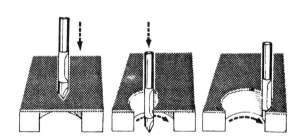

e Laminate pierce-and-trim

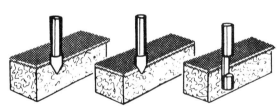

f Solid carbide cutter

Cutters for materials other than wood must be considered in the light of the increasing use of plastics, glassfibre and aluminium in the home and in industry.

Shaped burrs in solid carbide. Designed to cut glass-reinforced plastic, they can also be used for carving and shaping wood and abrasive plastics. Speeds are important – 25,000 rpm and below for wood; 10,000 to 40,000 rpm for metal; Fig 189A.

Glassfibre cutter. Used for cutting glass-reinforced plastic, but they can also be employed at speeds in excess of 10,000 rpm for de-burring and grinding metal; Fig 189B.

Acrylic cutter. Specially designed with close attention to the correct relief necessary for cutting materials such as Perspex, Orglas and Dexiglas; Fig 189C.

Aluminium cutter. For the grooving and milling of non-ferrous metals such as aluminium. They usually have two flutes; Fig 189D.

Aluminium and PVC cutter. Used for drilling and slotting aluminium and PVC extrusions. The cutters are manufactured in single, double and special three-flute designs; Fig 189E.

Engraving and vee-grooving cutter. For free-hand engraving, and for fine decorative work in wood. Ideal for model makers and engravers; Fig 189F.

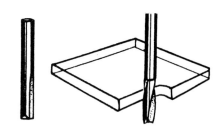

c Acrylic cutter with two flutes

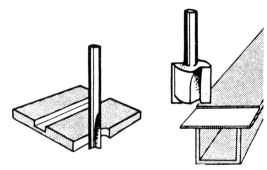

d Aluminium cutter

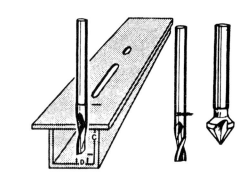

e Aluminium/PVC spiral-fluted cutter

189 *Miscellaneous Cutters*

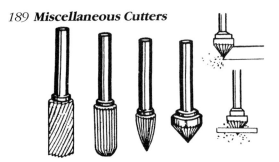

a Shaped burrs in solid carbide

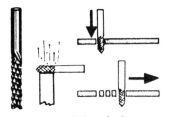

b Glassfibre cutter in solid carbide

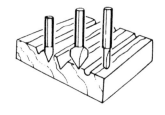

f Engraving and vee-grooving cutter

Special bits for boring as separate from router cutters. There are a number of boring bits which can be used in the router: such as plug cutters, saw-tooth Forstner bits and plain Forstner bits. They are available with short shanks sized to fit the router collet.

Hinge-sinkers for doors made in particle board. Special hinges are available for fitting to particle boards as distinct from the normal butt hinge. These special hinges usually require the accurate cutting of a hole to receive the barrel of the hinge. Since the boards are of material usually less than 25mm (1in), the bit must have a very small point to avoid the possibility of break-through. Hinge-sinkers are designed to bore in almost any material including plastic laminate boards and solid wood. For man-made material they must be made or tipped with tungsten-carbide.

Shaper rasps made in HSS can be used in high speed routers or power drills for cutting wood, plastics and non-ferrous metals. The shank diameter is 6mm (¼in), the ball is 14mm (⁹⁄₁₆in) diameter, while the others are 12mm by 30mm (½in by 1³⁄₁₆in). They are also available with 8mm (⁵⁄₁₆in) shanks.

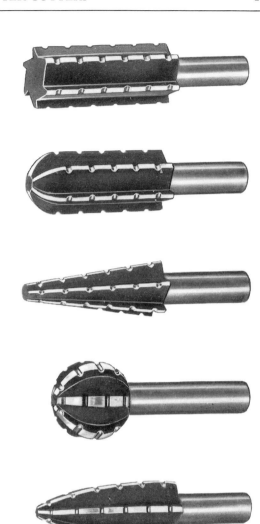

190 Hinge-sinking

191 Wolfcraft HSS shaper rasps

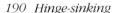
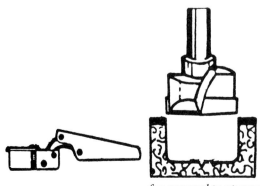
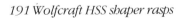
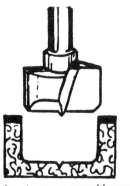

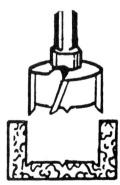

for general purposes   *for laminate-covered board*   *for wood or particle board*

Bits with disposable inserts. Throw away blades aren't a new idea, but the suggestion of applying the idea to router cutters and bits a few years back would probably have been received with derision.

The Versofix tools, however, have put paid to all that – they are disposable. Boring tools have always been an expensive item, but these will not only bore, plunging and routing come natural to them.

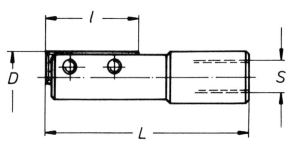

192 Versofix boring and routing tool with disposable inserts

They have a common shank available in three sizes, 10mm, 12mm, and 12.7mm (½in). Reverse inserts with ground-in chip breakers can be fitted to the shanks. These inserts are fitted in safety grooves with very close tolerances in setting; they give a fine, smooth, chip clearance, free from kick-back, so that they can safely be used in hand routers. They are plastic-coated for better chip flow, and each blade has two edges and can be sharpened. The blades are of a specially formulated steel, and not tungsten-carbide.

They would appear to be the answer to many boring problems.

Universal routing system. There are many developments taking place in router cutter and bit construction, but perhaps one of the most interesting ones is the Profiset system for use with portable routers. Built up router cutters have been largely used in the range of production routers, but here we have a system using router shanks of 6mm, 6.35mm (¼in), and 8mm.

Basically, this range consists of a router mandrel with a tool collet. Various cutters can be assembled to the mandrel – indeed, there are over forty different profiles which can be made up. These range from the simple single cutter to a more complicated multiple. At the same time, with the aid of ring spacers, the tool can be adjusted for any thickness of work piece. The mandrel can also be fitted with a self-guide bearing; and they can be bought in sets or purchased as single tools and the collection built up as the need arises. They are made with great accuracy, have tungsten-carbide tips with chip-thickness limitation, and are 'kick-back' proof. For any woodworker with a great variety of work applications, the Profiset system would seem to be the answer. Some of the combinations possible are illustrated; Fig 193.

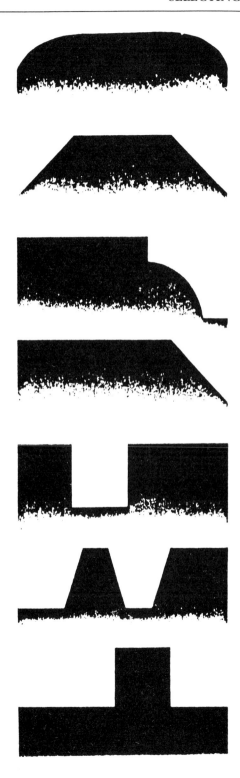

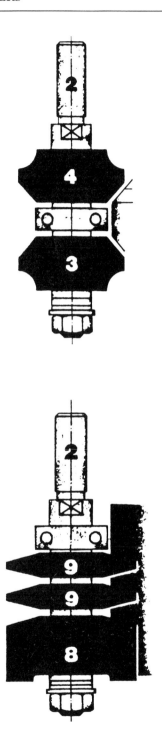

193 Profiset – built-up bonding set and profiles

194 Titman profiles

For those who work in the woodworking industry, there are many alternatives both in the style of cutter and the shape. Always refer to a well-known manufacturer's list. The following is taken from the Titman catalogue and there are many more.

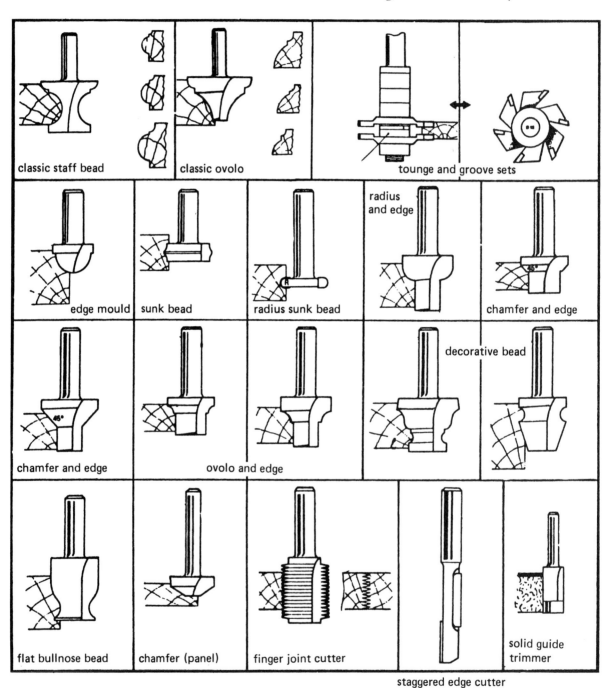

classic staff bead

classic ovolo

tounge and groove sets

edge mould

sunk bead

radius sunk bead

radius and edge

chamfer and edge

chamfer and edge

ovolo and edge

decorative bead

flat bullnose bead

chamfer (panel)

finger joint cutter

solid guide trimmer

staggered edge cutter

195 Profiles from KWO Tools Ltd

Further shapes come from KWO Tools Ltd.

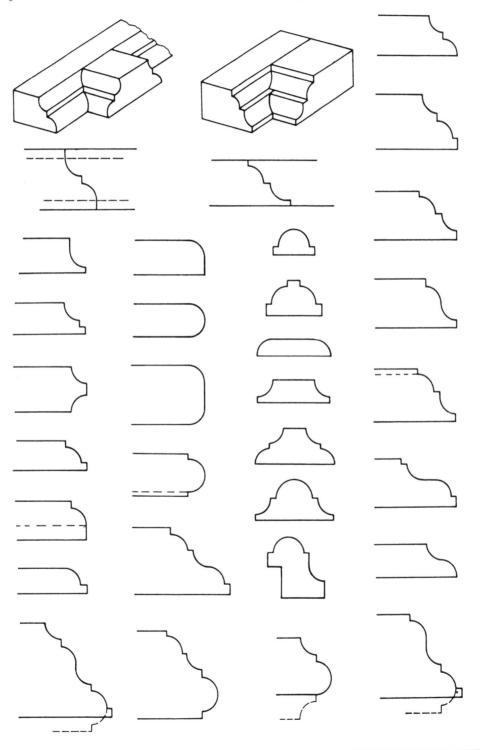

196　Profiles from Titman Tip Tools Ltd

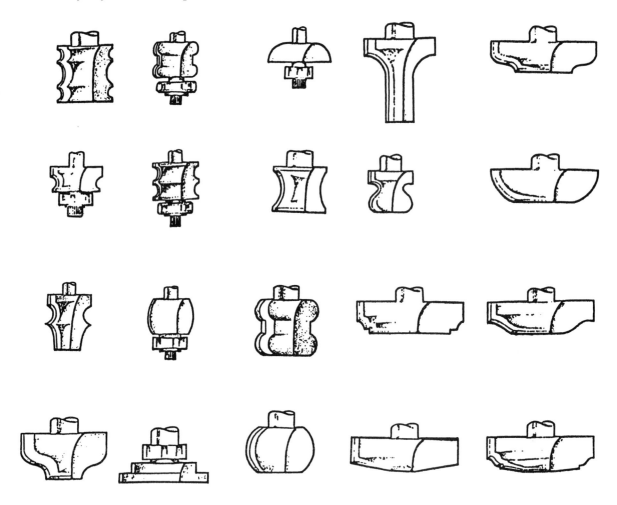

12 Router Cutter Maintenance

Too much emphasis cannot be placed on the need to keep all the cutters sharp; as sharp tools will ensure excellence of finish, and avoid overloading of the router.

All router cutters are carefully machined to exact shapes and tolerances and these must be preserved. Grinding is impossible without the use of quite complicated machinery, and when this becomes necessary the user is advised to return the cutters either to the manufacturer, or to a company specialising in the work. Limited sharpening can be carried out on HSS cutters, and even TCT, if diamond-slurry sharpening is available, but once again great care must be exercised to maintain shape and clearance.

Sharpening by using hand-held oil stones or slip-stones carefully held in a wood block or vice, is always done on the inside of the cutters to preserve

198 Sharpening a TCT cutter using the diamond-slurry system – tile held in the vice

197 Parts of the router cutter

a Ovolo with solid guide pin

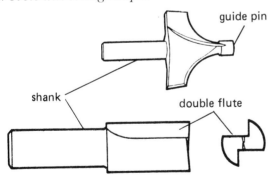

b Two-flute straight cutter

c Single-flute straight cutter

199 Hand-held sharpening with the slurry system

the tool size. Never touch the outside, otherwise the rake may be altered, and as a result the performance of the cutter will be impaired. Regular touching-up is always advisable; either carry it out before or after use. At the latter stage, touching-up will also help in removing resin or other fouling which, in the end, will retard the performance of the cutter. Once the sharpening bevel begins to round over or lose its shape, the cutter must be sent for grinding. Many of the suppliers of router cutters provide a service, and, bearing in mind the high cost of the cutters, it's best to send them to the experts.

Sharpening. The best method to use for most of the cutters is to mount a rectangular oilstone in a wood-working vice, edgewise up, or with the oilstone in a

200 Sharpening a cutter with the oilstone placed edge-up in the vice

201 a Oilstone holder with formica face

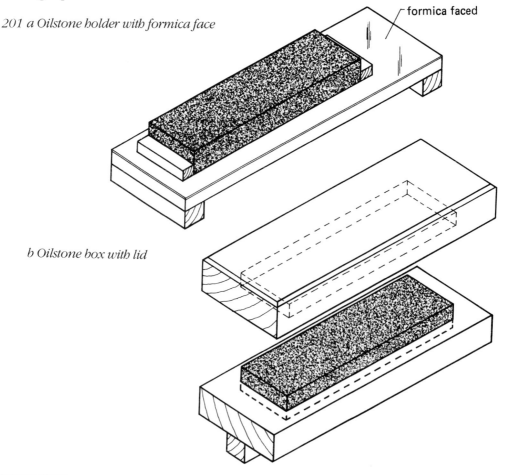

formica faced

b Oilstone box with lid

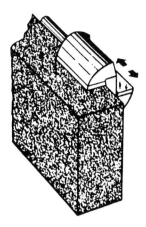
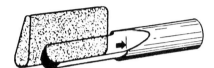

202 Sharpening
a Two-flute straight cutter
b A single-flute cutter with a slipstone
c The ovolo fitted with a guide pin

wood block which is held similarly. Hold the cutter between the finger and thumb, and place the flute over the corner of the stone, after first lightly oiling the stone with a thin non-drying oil (3 in 1 is one in common use).

Rub the cutter backwards and forwards, keeping it firmly in position so that it does not rock. Most cutters have an included angle of 90°, and if the angle of the oil stone is accurate a fine edge can be quickly obtained on HSS cutters. A slip-stone can be used lightly to remove the burr which will appear on the edge, but great care is needed not to rub too hard and so alter the shape. Slipstones can be obtained in a variety of sizes and radii to suit. Perhaps the best type of tool to use to remove this burr is a rubberised slip-stone which will give an added bonus of polish to the cutter.

203 Sharpening a cutter on a rubberised block held in the vice

204 Sharpening a cutter with the rubberised block held in the hand

205 *Wood block bored and split to hold router cutters for sharpening*

Panel cutters with single flutes should be gripped lightly in a small vice (at a pinch they could be hand-held), or a wooden block can be cut which will grip the cutter in a vee-cut before the block is placed in a vice. The cutter can be sharpened in its flute, using a hard slip-stone or the rubberised version. Once again, remove the burr with care.

Tungsten-carbide tipped, and solid carbide cutters, can have limited sharpening in the same way, but the purchase of a diamond sharpening stick is necessary. The author has used a plastic stick dressed with diamond slurry to carry out this limited sharpening.

Care. Keep the cutters free from resin and other fouling. This may be removed with sharpening, but it is advisable to keep a can of cleaning fluid handy to clean the cutter after use. The build-up of fouling can result in decreased efficiency of the cutter itself, poor chip clearance, and, as a result, an increase in frictional burning. A badly maintained cutter will, of course, need greater effort from the operator with consequent overloading of the router itself.

Attention must also be paid to keeping the guide pins and self-guide bearings free from fouling; they should always be kept in a polished condition. Examination immediately after use will invariably show up any fouling, particularly after cutting many of the plastic laminates.

Never keep the bits in a box – always in stands so that they will not be in contact with each other and possibly be damaged. Lightly wipe the cutter with an oily rag before storing. Many router cutters come ready-packed in plastic storage cases, so keep them in these. Alternatively, use one of the proprietary brands of protective spray coatings.

It must be constantly borne in mind that cutters subjected to damp conditions will rust, and deep rust will cause the quick break-down of sharpened edges.

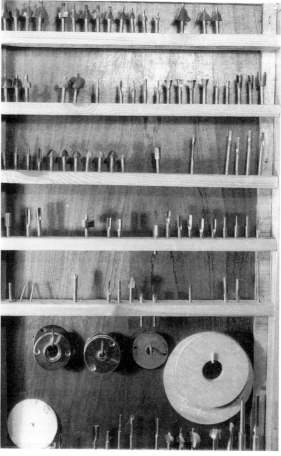

206 *Router cutter storage*

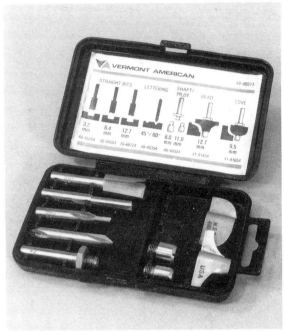

208 Router cutter set in hard plastic case

207 Router cutter stands

There is a number of sharpening and grinding attachments available, but the reader is advised to examine them carefully before purchase and match the cost against the volume of sharpening which is required. Using machine attachments of this kind can often result in over-grinding and the total loss of the cutter. When using router cutters with inter-changeable shanks, care must be taken to hold the cutter shank by means of the flats provided for this purpose. Always use a spanner or a small vice with plain jaws to hold the cutter, and never hold it by its shank.

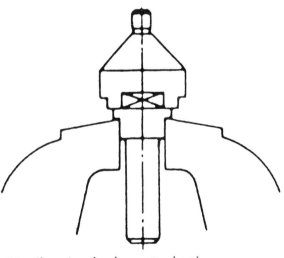

209 Changing shank or cutter head

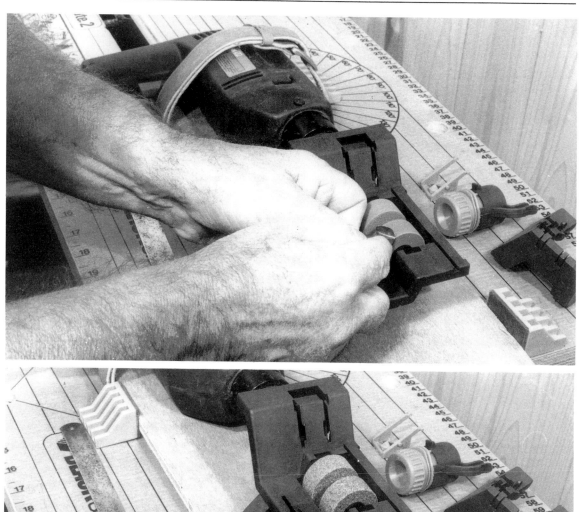

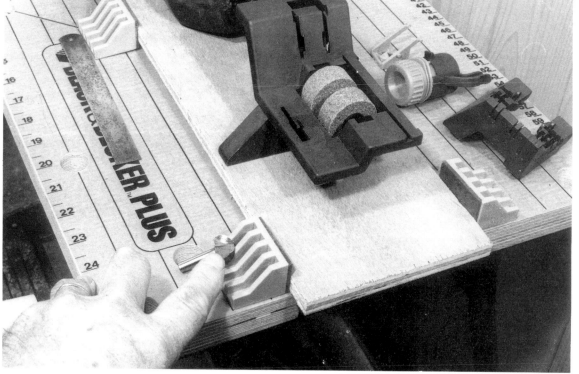

Cutter sharpening attachments. Grinding router cutters is fraught with difficulty as they are precisely made, and the shapes and clearances must be retained if the cutter is to give satisfactory service. At the same time HSS and TCT cutters require different types of grinding grits. Limited grinding can be carried out, but care is the watch word.

A small attachment for the electric power drill is available and this is called the Attracta Multi-sharp. Although it can be used with a small additional attachment for drill grinding, it is only in the straightforward grinder position that it can be used with router cutters. A green wheel is fitted at the right hand side of the attachment, and this is the one to use for grinding tungsten-carbide tipped cutters.

The attachment is best fixed to a piece of blockboard on which the drill will rest when fitted; have a good light on the job; make sure that the assembly is firmly held and use good goggles to protect the eyes.

210 Attracta drill attachment-sharpening a TCT cutter on the green wheel

211 Sharpening completed

13 Router Maintenance

The use of oil lubrication must be strictly limited to a light wipe of the sliding columns of the plunge mechanisms. Keep the router clean, and whenever timber with resin, oil, grease, or other secretions has been worked on the user will be wise to clean the machine immediately after use. Use a suitable solvent for this; there are several good proprietary cleaners on the market. Any fouling can be harmful for the router, and often makes traversing and movement difficult.

Check all screws and fittings for security from time to time. Unusual noise or vibration should be dealt with immediately. Switch the router off, and first check the router cutter for distortion or chipped edges, which may be the cause. If not, proceed to a close examination of the router spindle by first removing the collet nut and jaws. Grip the spindle firmly and turn it to see if it rotates easily. Try moving the spindle from side to side to test for slackness; follow through with an upward thrust and a downward pull to detect any movement. If in doubt, take the router to a service centre; do not attempt repairs yourself.

It's a good idea to use the blowing end of the vacuum cleaner (if it is the type which allows this to be done) to blow out the dust. It's surprising how much fine dust can accumulate in the router.

Read the maker's instructions regarding the care of the router, as designs vary and changes are made which you may not be aware of.

A constant check must be kept on the collet; look particularly for wear since this can mean ill-fitting cutters, leading to looseness and danger. Keep the threads clean and remember that timber dust can create fouling around this area, and in the end cause trouble.

Should the collet be suspect, examine a cutter to see if there are any marks on its shank which might give an indication of wear. Take a brand-new cutter, insert it in the collet and tighten up by hand. Hold the cutter at its cutting end (taking care not to cut

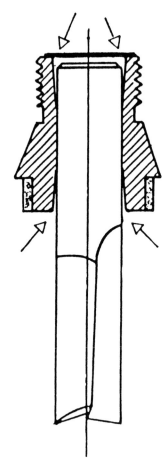

212 The collet – checking for wear

your finger), and see if there is any movement from side to side. If there is excessive movement, replace with a new collet.

Keep a keen eye on the router cutters for sharpness. Limited sharpening can be carried out in the workshop as outlined in the Sharpening section (see page 122). Badly-chipped cutters will need re-grinding, and this should be done by an expert, as grinding angles and clearances are critical if the router cutter is to work perfectly.

LOOK AND LISTEN MUST BE THE RULE FOR ADEQUATE MAINTENANCE.

Electrics – the essentials

Most power tools these days have double insulation incorporated in the body design, but this should not encourage complacency on the part of the user. There are a number of points to which attention must be paid to avoid electric shock, fire, and consequent injury from either.

First check that the supply voltage shown on the machine is the same as in the workshop. It should be within plus or minus 10%; that is, a 220 volt machine will be quite safe to use on a 240 volt supply. Many European machines are fitted with two-pin plugs. If the router is to be used on a purpose-designed bench, then the socket which is often supplied with the bench will be the correct type to receive it, and the switch will be the no-volt release safety type. A two or three-pin fused adaptor, (the three-pin being the 13amp type), can be used; alternatively, the European plug can be removed and replaced with a 13amp three-pin plug if a bench is not to be used. Similar problems will arise in the USA and can be resolved in the same way.

To fit a new plug; prepare the cable ends by removing a small length of the insulation; if the router has only two wires these should be connected Brown (or Red) to the live terminal, Blue (or Black) to the negative terminal. The three wire system will have a yellow and green wire which must run to the earth terminal. Screw down securely on each terminal, replace the cover, then tighten down on the two screws which serve to hold the cable tightly.

220/240 volt tools should always be protected with a 13amp fuse. If a 115 volt tool is to be used and the rating of the tool is under 1500 watts, a 15amp fuse should be used, and a 20amp fuse for 1500 watts or more.

Care must also be exercised when selecting extension cables – don't use just any old extension – indeed, it is sensible to buy one which is supplied, or recommended by, the maker of the router. If in doubt get some advice about this from a reputable tool dealer.

Conductor sizes. For cables rated at 6amp use a conductor size of 0.75mm: 10amp – 1mm: 15amp – 1.5mm: 20amp – 2.5mm: 25amp – 4mm.

Cable rating	Conductor size
6amps	0.75mm
10amps	1.00mm
15amps	1.50mm
20amps	2.50mm
25amps	4.00mm

Extension Cable Rating

Tool Voltage Amps (on nameplate)		Extension cable length - Metres					
		7 5	15	25	30	45	60
		Cable Rating-Amperes					
115	0 - 2 0	6	6	6	6	6	10
	2 1 - 3 4	6	6	6	6	15	15
	3 5 - 5 0	6	6	10	15	20	20
	5 1 - 7 0	10	10	15	20	20	25
	7 1 - 12 0	15	15	20	25	25	
	12 1 - 20 0	20	20	25			
220/ 240	0 - 2 0	6	6	6	6	6	6
	2 1 - 3 4	6	6	6	6	6	6
	3 5 - 5 0	6	6	6	6	10	15
	5 1 - 7 0	10	10	10	10	15	15
	7 1 - 12 0	15	15	15	15	20	20
	12 1 - 20 0	20	20	20	20	25	

213 Extension cable rating table

Take care never to subject the motor to damp, moisture, or oil, and never expose the windings to the possibility of damage.

Check the carbon brushes periodically and replace them before they become so worn as to damage the commutator of the motor (ie, if less than 6mm in length). Fitting new carbon brushes is very easy and they are readily available. It's a good plan when buying your router to buy a spare pair. Usually

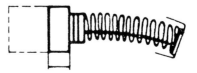

6 mm (1/4″)

214 Carbon brush and spring

*215 Changing the brushes
on an Hitachi – unscrewing*

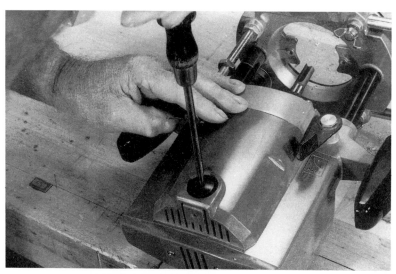

216 Examining the brush

the brushes are reached through an aperture in the body, and a small flush-fitting screw indicates their position. Unscrew this, carefully draw out the spring and brush – they are normally attached to one another. Should the brushes be less than 6mm (¼in) in length, replace them with new ones. Always change both brushes, and never use ones of odd lengths. If the brushes are serviceable, give them a good clean and replace them carefully in the same position. The curve on the commutator brushes must be perfectly matched to it and not altered during cleaning.

14 Materials

Materials can be divided into:
a. softwoods, b. hardwoods, c. man-made boards, d. non-ferrous metals, and e. plastics.

Care must always be exercised in the choice of cutter for the kind of material being worked. Mistakes can be expensive, and often the inexperienced user will regard all timber as just timber, thereby failing to appreciate the great variation in degrees of hardness in particular, and also the problems associated with resin, oil, and other materials which can in themselves be destructive of edges, or inhibit the smooth progress of the router over the work.

Softwoods can generally be cut with HSS cutters; indeed, unless they are extremely knotty they will not require the harder TCT or tungsten-carbide type. There can be, however, a very high resin content in the timber, and the cutters must be cleaned regularly otherwise a build-up of resin on the edges will cause cutting breakdown. A really tough softwood such as yew, may well have to be classed as a hardwood when cutters are being selected for it.

Hardwoods can generally be cut with HSS cutters, but the very hard ones will need TCT or tungsten-carbide cutters.

Man-made boards, such as particle board (chipboard and medium-density fibreboard (MDF)), have a very high content of extremely hard glue, wood chips or granules of varying degrees of hardness, and some grit. All three factors will quickly lead to a breakdown of the edges if the wrong kind of cutter is employed, and TCT cutters must be used. This also applies to plywood, blockboard, laminboard, and similar materials since once again they are bonded with extremely hard glue and often contain a great variety of timbers in their composition.

Non-ferrous metals like aluminium require a careful choice of cutters, since the angles of cutting differ – as also do the clearance angles. The reader would be well advised to seek guidance from a specialist supplier, particularly if a great deal of work is to be carried out. Solid plastics, and boards faced with plastic laminates, all require TCT cutters.

A number of reputable manufacturers are tackling the problems associated with cutting different materials by plastic-coating the cutters or bits to give better chip flow. There is also a move to offer cutters with disposable tips; these have no tungsten content, but are specially designed and made from a material formulated to give increased performance. Both of the foregoing will greatly ease the problems associated with man-made materials in particular. Diamond-tipped cutters are undoubtedly the ultimate, but are generally excluded for most users on the grounds of cost.

The underlying thought must be, that although the router itself may be reasonable in price, it's the cutters that run away with the money. Thus, knowledgeable selection must be the operative words to reduce the high cost of tooling.

Information on timber and timber products can be obtained from:

Timber Research and Development Association
Hughenden Valley
High Wycombe
Bucks HP14 4ND

Forest Products Laboratory
Forest Service
US Department of Agriculture
Madison
Wisconsin

15 Joints and Other Cuts

Most of the joints used in cabinet construction can be made using the router, but in many cases a jig of some kind is needed. These can be quite simple in the case of the mortise and tenon joint, but a little more complicated when dovetailing is undertaken. Undoubtedly, great accuracy can be obtained, and the speeding up of the work is a real bonus.

The stub mortise and tenon is most commonly used in simple frame and stool construction.

The sloping haunch mortise and tenon is used to secure the top rail in table and stool work. The haunch ensures a total engagement of the rail in the mortise without the tenon coming through at the top of the leg; Fig 218A.

The square haunch mortise and tenon is the joint used in a framework, with a groove cut to house a plywood or solid panel. The square haunch allows for the through cutting of the groove with the router, and a haunch left on the rail fits neatly into it with all parts of the joint in contact with each other for maximum strength; Fig 218B.

The long and short-shouldered mortise and tenon must be used in cases where the frame houses either a panel of timber or a sheet of glass held in place with a small beading. In this joint, not only do we see the square haunch, but also that the rear shoulder is forward of the front shoulder by the depth of the rebate. This ensures the coming together of both shoulders to make a perfect joint; Fig 218C.

The dovetail bridle joint. Used in frames without panels, and in a number of other cabinet joints. Also employed on picture frames; Fig 218D.

The dowelled joint is usually associated with various types of dowelling jigs which can be easily made with the plunge router; Fig 218E.

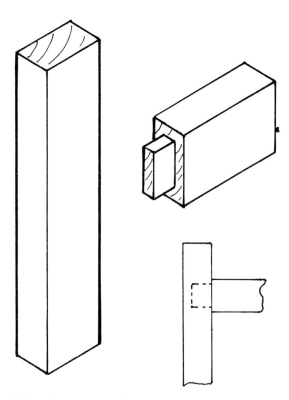

217 Stub mortise and tenon

218

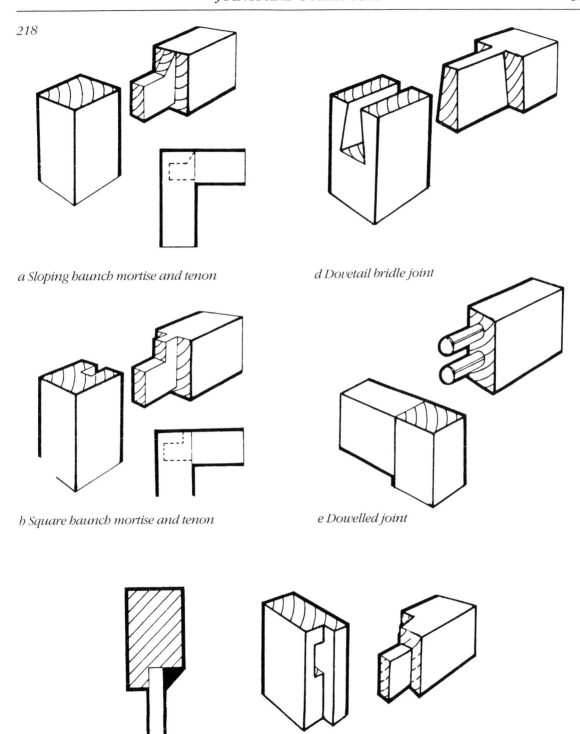

a Sloping haunch mortise and tenon

d Dovetail bridle joint

b Square haunch mortise and tenon

e Dowelled joint

c Long and short-shouldered mortise and tenon

The through-dovetail or common dovetail joint. The dovetail joint presents a number of problems if cut entirely by hand, but these are removed with the introduction of dovetailing jigs of various kinds. The through dovetail is widely used in box and cabinet construction, and where the sizes of the pins and sockets can be varied it makes a very attractive and decorative joint.

The lapped dovetail or stopped dovetail joint is particularly needed where the joint must not be seen, as when it joins the front and the sides of a drawer. It is, however, used by many craftsmen in numerous other constructions, and like the through-dovetailed joint can become an attractive feature of the design.

The finger joint. A very commonly used joint in commercial box construction; not quite as strong as the dovetail but adequate for constructions where strength is not the primary factor.

The housing or dado (in the USA) joint is usually associated with the making of bookcases and shelving units. Shelves are inserted in grooves cut across the grain, the name housing or dado distinguishing them from grooves which run with the grain.

219

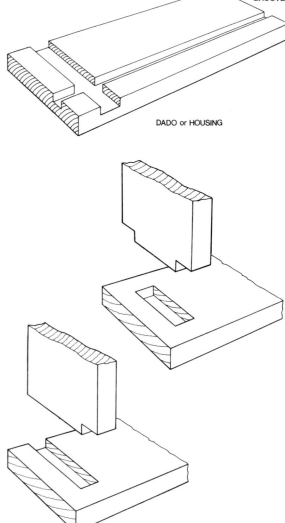

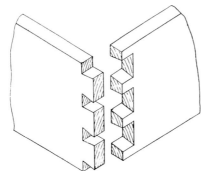

a Through or common dovetail joint

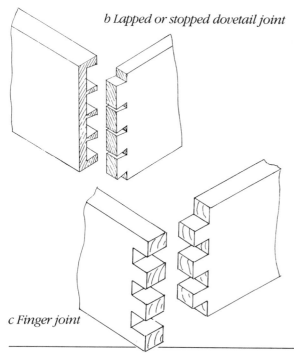

b Lapped or stopped dovetail joint

c Finger joint

d Housing or dado joint

Tiled wall clock, routed caricature, and meatboard

Stopped housings are never cut completely across in order to avoid seeing the cut on the face of the work. They are stopped at a point close to the face edge.

Double-stopped housing. In free-standing units where the joints would otherwise be seen on both faces, a double-stopped housing is used.

Stopped groove joint. This is well suited to being cut with the router. Grooves are cut on both legs and rails and a tongue (spline in the USA) of hardwood is inserted and glued to unite them. It is essential that the grain of the tongue should be at 90° to the grain of the legs.

Stopped groove and rebate joint. This is similar to the previous joint, but a groove is cut in the leg and the rebate in the rail forms a barefaced tenon.

Board joint, or groove and loose tongue. One joint which can be used in the jointing of narrow boards, consisting of two grooves with an inserted tongue. The best type of tongue is made from hardwood, the short grain running at 90° to the grain of the timber being joined. Alternatively, multi-plywood can be utilised and this makes an extremely strong joint.

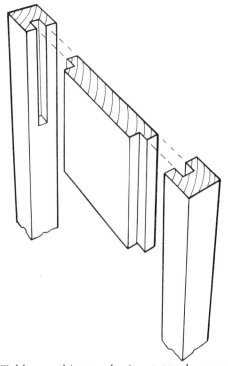

221 Table or cabinet end using stopped groove and rebate

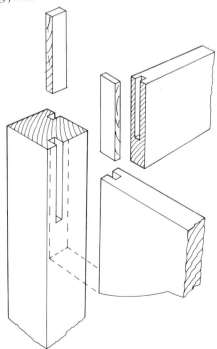

220 Table construction using the stopped groove joint

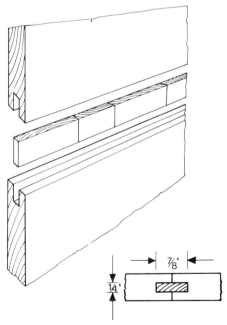

222 a Tongued jointing of boards
b Size of the tongue

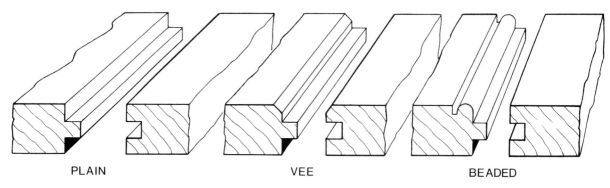

PLAIN   VEE   BEADED

223 Tongued and grooved jointing of boards for door construction

Tongued and grooved jointing of boards for door making, wall boarding and fence making. The joint consists of a groove into which the tongue of the adjacent board fits. Manufactured boards usually have a vee-cut on the tongued edge or a bead, both purely for appearance. Variations on these two patterns can be made using the router and other profiles of router cutters.

Hinge housings. Not recesses or joints in the strict sense, although the joining of a door to a frame needs the accurate recessing of the hinge in both door and frame. This is called a 'gain' in the USA but is usually referred to in the UK as a recess or housing. Easily cut with the router using a template and guide.

Rebated corner joint. This joint will facilitate the making of drawers and cabinets. It consists simply of a rebate cut along the edge of the full thickness of the timber at each end of both the bottom and top pieces in the case of a cabinet, the width of the rebate being equal to the full thickness of the side members, which are then glued and pinned. The joint can also be used to join the front of a drawer to the sides. If a rounding-over or similar cutter is used, a very acceptable finish can be given to the work.

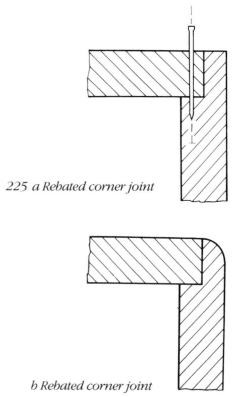

225 a Rebated corner joint

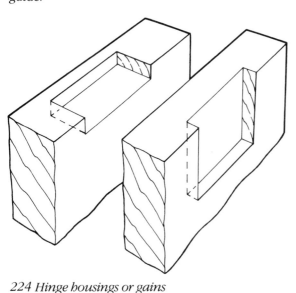

224 Hinge housings or gains

b Rebated corner joint

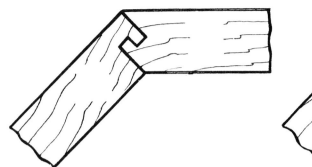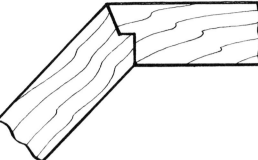

226 Mitred corners

Mitred joints. A small jig will have to be made to position the router, so that the groove can be cut on the 45° mitre. A tongue is used to complete the joint. See making a box pages 140-1.

Alternatively, if the mitres are placed back to back and cramped temporarily while being cut, they will make up an angle of 90° to enable cutting to be carried out using the straight fence.

Other Corner Joints. The router with its many shapes of cutter opens up a wide range of options in cabinets and table construction. Corner joints for solid wood cabinets can be made using a rebate and the corners completed with a rounding-over cutter, an ovolo, or any suitable edge-shaping cutter.

Table construction, using legs and rails, can incorporate a number of variations of joint and decorative treatments.

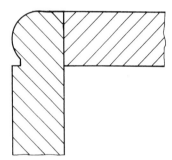

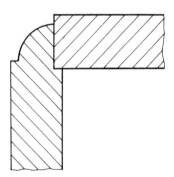

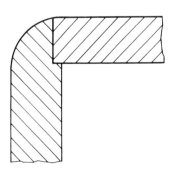

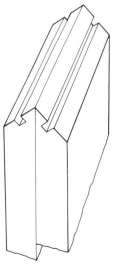

227 Mitres placed back to back for grooving

228 Corner joints

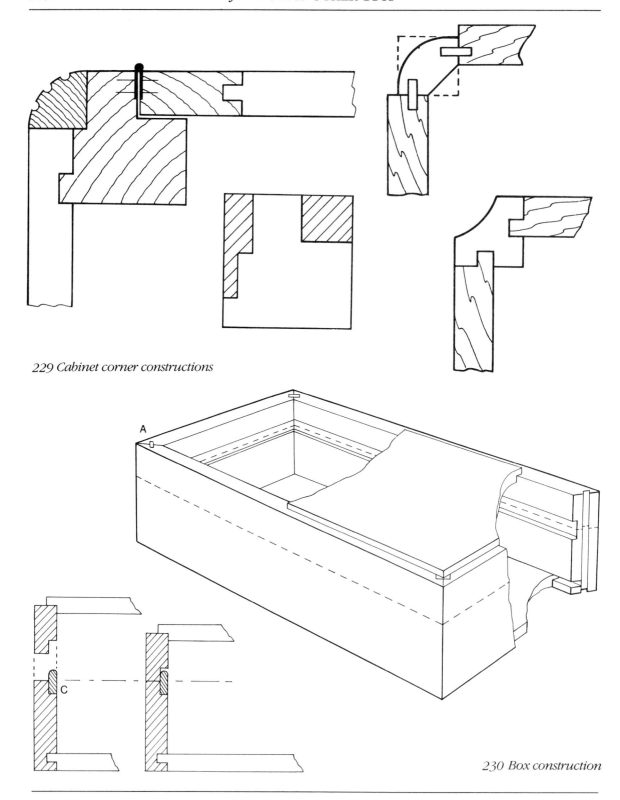

229 Cabinet corner constructions

230 Box construction

Box Construction. Box corners can be mitred, then grooved with the router and joined with a tongue. Both the base and the lid can be rebated. Alternatively, the base can be rebated to form a tongue which is inserted in a groove cut in the box sides.

If the box requires a sliding lid, the lid can be uncut and slide in a groove cut in the box sides. Alternatively a rebate may be cut to form a tongue and the lid inserted to run flush with the sides of the box or in reverse with the rebated side on the inside of the box.

Another joint for the box corners is the rebate and groove; the only problem here is that the short end grain on the grooved part of the joint may be unsightly and liable to damage.

An unhinged box lid can be positioned using a beading planted in a rebate on the inside top edge of the box. The beading can be rounded over using a suitable cutter.

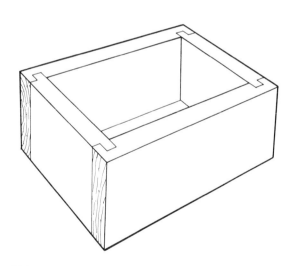

231 Box construction

CABINET DOOR MAKING

This has changed greatly with the introduction of the router and with the design of mass-production machines using similar cutters to those used in the hand-held portable router. Hopefully, the majority of my readers will still find the challenge of making doors in the traditional style stimulating. At the same time, the router can be brought in to add a great variety of cuts and mouldings which in fact could not be done without either a large number of the old-fashioned moulding planes or one of the more modern multiplanes, and the line drawings show a number of different treatments.

Generally the door frame will be made using the long and short-shouldered mortise and tenon joint (see page 148) if the panel is to be held in a rebate. If the panel is to be grooved in the joint will be the square haunched mortise and tenon; the groove is generally cut the same width as the tenon itself.

232 Cabinet door making

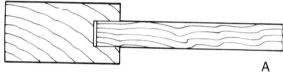

A

a Here a groove is cut with the router using a straight panel bit. This is the most simple style.

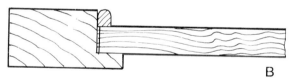

B

b Uses a rebate cut with a router bit, the panel being held in place with a loose bead which is held in place with panel pins. The loose beading can be rounded over with a bit passed through a specially made tunnel which fits to the fence of a router bench (see page 56) in order to support the thin material as it passes the router bit.

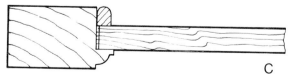

C

c After the joints are cut the ovolo cutter is used to cut an ovolo along the inside face of the four pieces. A rebate is then cut with a straight bit. The panel is once again held in place with a loose bead.

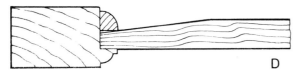

D

d Similar to c, but in this case the panel is held in the rebate by material of quadrant section shaped with a rounding-over bit.

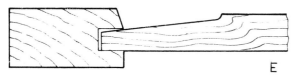

E

e A straightforward groove is used to hold the panel, but both panel and face of the frame have been shaped with the router. This treatment can be carried out with profile cutters but these are extremely expensive and require a heavy duty router.

Meeting door edges. Where a cabinet has two doors meeting at the centre, it is usual to cut a rebate on one door edge on the inside, and to cut a bead with a beading cutter on the outside. The other door has a matching rebate cut in its edge. Both doors are, of course, made correspondingly wider to allow for the width of the rebate; Fig 233A.

A simpler method is to plant a decorative strip on the edge of one door to lap over the edge on the other to form a simple closing strip. Any one of a number of different shapes could be applied here, depending on the range of router cutters available; Fig 233B.

A strip, first rebated and then rounded over on the front, is perhaps an improvement on the planted one; Fig 233C.

A simple and often used method of masking the joint of two meeting doors is shown in Fig 233D.

233 Double-door edge treatments A,B,C,D

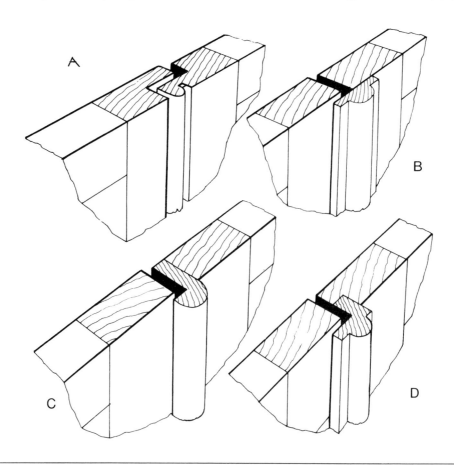

234 Drawer-making

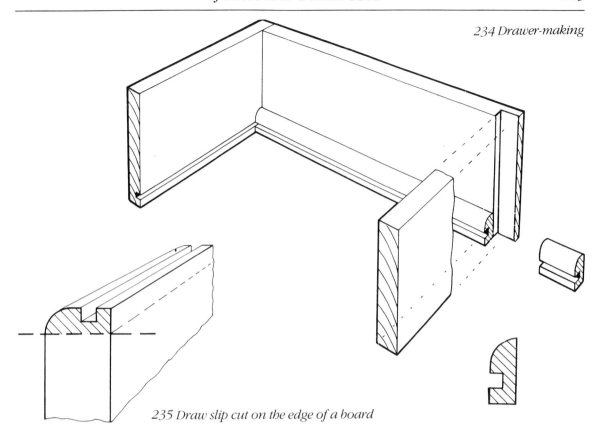

235 Draw slip cut on the edge of a board

DRAWER-MAKING

After the preparation of the timber, the complete business of drawer making can be tackled with the router.

There are two ways of jointing the front corners; either the straightforward housing as previously described, or by lapped dovetails. The latter construction is shown on page 134. The important thing is that the joint must not be seen from the front although the craftsman may even reject this, particularly when perfection is attainable using one of the dovetail jigs, the dovetail can then be used as a decorative feature in the cabinet design.

The back is usually housed in a groove which can be cut with a straight router cutter. An alternative is to cut an open housing as suggested for the front; the back being glued and pinned into it. If the drawer back can be brought forward, then a full housing can be used instead.

Usually the drawer bottom slides in a groove which passes under the back and is secured by pinning into the underside of the back. An alternative to the groove is a slip into which a groove is made with the straight router cutter. This is then pinned in place. This suggestion is particularly important when the timber is fairly thin and the cutting of a groove may seriously weaken the side members.

Very wide drawers may require a joint in the material used in the bottom, and the problem can be solved by using a centre slip.

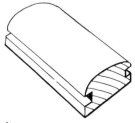

236 Centre slip

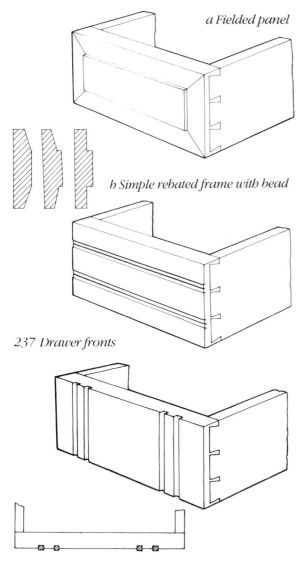

a Fielded panel

b Simple rebated frame with bead

237 Drawer fronts

b Material edged with cocked beads

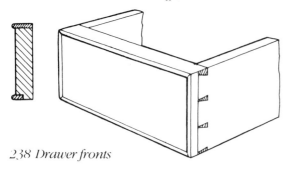

238 Drawer fronts

The easiest way to make the slips is to cut them on the edge of a board and slice them through with the circular saw. A suitable tunnel can be made and attached to the fence of the router table and the thin material can be pushed through. See page 56.

Some very attractive drawer fronts can be made using router cutters to work the designs, using straight cutting tools. If fielded panel cutters are available a number of variations can be made.

Very thin line inlays can be made in a variety of different timbers.

Vertical cocked beads will serve to break the line of long drawers. Again, the cocked beads can be made in the router table tunnel or cut on the edge of a board and sliced off.

If particle board or other man-made boards have to be used, the edges can be completed by the addition of a cocked bead.

JOINTING CABINET BACKS

Backs were made in solid wood in much of the furniture of the past, as there was no alternative. Certainly, nailing on plywood panels is frowned upon today, and many craftsmen prefer to make light frames and fit plywood panels into them; the completed panels are then carefully screwed in place.

The diagram shows a simple treatment for this – just a grooved panel with plywood set in; Fig 239A.

Solid panels can have a decorative bead as in Fig 239B.

Panels can be joined and supported in rebated material; Fig 239C, D, and E.

Another method is to insert a frame into the back of the cabinet and hold the plywood panel in place with a beading, cut with an ovolo or similar shape of cutter.

CUTTING MORTISES

There are a number of methods for cutting mortises, depending on the equipment available and, to a certain extent, the ingenuity of the craftsman.

One of the best methods I have used, particularly in the making of mortises in table and stool legs, is to make a box guide as shown. This is made in multi-plywood slightly thicker than the depth of the

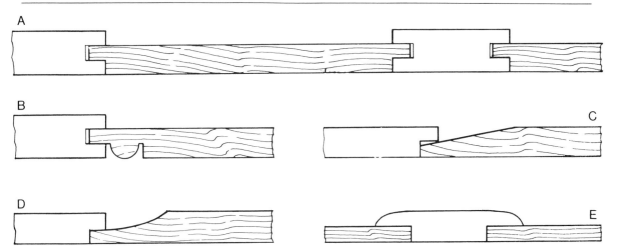

239 A to E – panelling of cabinet backs

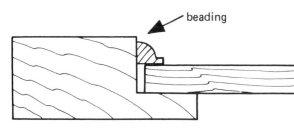

240 Back held in rebated frame using a bead

241 Stool leg dropped into plywood jig

chosen router guide bush. Since there are four mortises to each leg, two guide slots are cut taking the measurements from the upper and lower rails. Where the mortise is centrally placed in the leg, one template only will be required, but in cases where the mortises are closer to the edge (in other words, offset) a template with recesses cut at both ends with a common one at the centre for the lower mortise in each leg will be needed to give positional accuracy. A stop is fitted at one end of the box in the case of the single type, and at both ends in the double box. Refer to Chapter 10 for details needed to cut the template.

Take care to plane and cut the timber accurately to size and place a face-side and a face-edge mark on each piece; these will be the only marks needed. A cross to indicate the approximate position of each mortise will prevent the cutting of mortises in the wrong position.

Place a leg into the guide box against the stop; then put this assembly into the vice. Make certain that the vice is tight so that it will hold the box and also the leg within it. The box is put together using panel pins which allow for some degree of squeezing, thereby ensuring a positive hold.

Set up the router with a guide bush of the correct size, and insert the panel router cutter into the collet. Position the depth gauge and check everything before starting to cut. Plug in the router; place it in position with the guide bush located in the slot of the template; switch on the machine; plunge the cutter, and move instantly along the slot moving forward and to the right as the cutter rotates. Complete the cutting, retract the cutter, and wait for the motor to stop before removing the router. Move to the lower

242 Both mortises cut

slot and follow the same procedure. Repeat until all mortises have been cut.

In the case of the offset mortises, care must be taken to check every time that the mortises will be cut nearest to the marked face of each leg.

Generally, when making tables and stools and similar pieces, the haunches are sloped, this must be done by hand using a chisel of correct width.

Another method

Where a router table is available a guide block, cut from suitable timber, must be made and attached to the table fence using a G-cramp. It will not only position each piece for the accurate location of each mortise, but also will guide the timber down on to the router cutter. A mark on the side of the wood block indicates the start of the mortise, and the block itself stops the forward movement of the timber and so limits the length of the mortise.

Set up the table, and have the panel cutter to suit the size of the mortise inserted in the router collet. Set the depth gauge to give the correct depth of mortise by measuring from the table top to take into account the table thickness. Mark a clear pencil line on the table top to coincide with the centre of the router cutter. This mark will line up with the stop block start-mark previously mentioned. Cramp the block in place.

Take the piece to be mortised, line it up with the start-line on the block, and gently slide it down on to the router cutter. The block is deep enough to allow this to take place without any chance of the work piece being moved sideways by the action of the rotating cutter. Allow the cutter to pierce to its full depth before pushing the work up to the stop on the block. This method permits the mortise to be cut to the full width, length, and depth, all in one setting. The bench fence can be used to make changes in settings according to the width of the timber, and a series of stop blocks can be used to suit different thicknesses.

If a Wolfcraft Electronic Drill Stand or similar is available, it can be used to cut mortises, and where these have to be haunched this can also be done.

The Morten Jig is purpose-designed to simplify the making of mortise and tenon joints. This jig simplifies the making of single and multiple mortise and tenon joints at any angle with extreme accuracy.

*243 Cutting a mortise
    another way using
    a table jig*

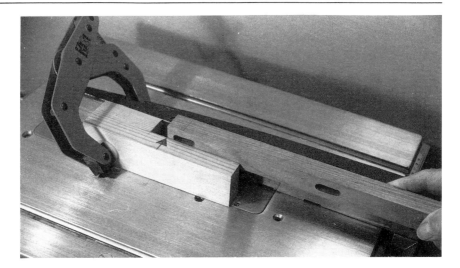

244 Mortise completed

It consists of a metal guide plate to which wood stops can be fitted.

The jig is made for cutting both tenons and mortises, using a 6.35mm (¼in) straight cutter fitted with a self-guide bearing.

The template and the work piece are cramped together with a G-cramp, and the complete assembly is then held in the bench vice. The mortise can be cut first; then the template is flipped over for cutting the tenon.

Make the necessary settings to the router, and check that the bearing will run smoothly along the template edge, and also that the cutter is clear of the template edge. Rest the router with its forward edge only resting on the jig, switch it on and carefully tilt it so that the cutter enters the timber and the router base is finally flat on the jig. Plunge fully, then move the router carefully around the mortise hole. When complete, switch off and wait for the router to stop. Similarly, the tenon can be cut with the jig flipped

245 Porter Cable Morten jig for cutting mortise and tenon joints

246 Cutting a mortise using two fences on the router

over; this time moving the router around the work piece following the jig as previously.

Perhaps one of the easiest methods used to cut mortises is to use the router fitted with its straight fence. The fence is set at the required depth of the tenon shoulder, and the depth stop at the specified depth of the mortise. Pencil marks to indicate start and stop positions – which in turn define the required length of the mortise – are made on the work piece so that they can be seen through the base of the router. When all the settings have been made, place the router flat on the work piece at the indicated point of start, switch it on, hold the fence firmly against the job, and plunge carefully to the full depth. This may not be possible with some routers, which may be underpowered; experience will tell you this and in the event you may have to make several passes. At full plunge, push the router forward and come to a stop at the indicated position; allow the router to stop fully before removing it. This method requires a little practice, particularly at sighting the start and stop positions.

One point to be remembered with mortises cut with the router: they are always round-shaped at the ends. Some craftsmen round over the tenons to fit, while others square up the ends of the mortises. Either method is satisfactory, but probably the easier is to round the tenons, as the correct size mortise chisel may not be readily available.

Cutting tenons

The Morten jig from the Porter Cable Company is one of the easiest to use for this job.

If a work table is available, the addition of one or two workshop-made jigs will simplify the making of tenons. I have added a table to the Triton work bench, and this is held in position on top of the lower table with a couple of G-cramps. To this table two stops have been pinned; one (A) to limit the length of the tenons, and the other (B) to position and act as a stop against which the pieces to be tenoned are located. These are marked and shown in Fig 247.

Rails have been prepared for the making of a table in three sets of four, planed accurately to size, and cut to exact length. Place four in position and cramp them together securely; the assembly may in turn be cramped to the sub-bench top.

Attach the router to the router sliding table, place

247 Cutting tenons on the Triton with the sub-table fitted

248 Completed table rails

a straight cutter in the collet, and set the depth stop so that a cut can be made to the depth of the shoulder of the tenon. Flip the sliding table over so that it will run in the recess on both sides of the Triton table. Switch on the router, and slide it over the work pieces; the stop will prevent the edge of the last piece from breaking out as well as serving as a stop. The diameter of the cutter will, of course, dictate the length of the tenons, and several cuts may have to be made to achieve longer tenons by moving the cramped pieces away from the stop by a sufficient amount. When complete, turn the pieces over and re-cramp them to cut the reverse side. Follow through with the remainder of the tenons.

Should the tenons need square haunching, set the tenoned pieces edge-on and re-set the router to the required depth of cut. Move the router carefully to avoid breakout, since the tenons will be entirely un-supported.

Another method is to use the Black & Decker Power Tool Table. Here, we need the use of the

249 Moving the clamped rails across the rotating cutter

250 Completed tenons

bevel fence which comes as standard with the table. The router is fitted with a suitable straight cutter which is set to cut to the depth of the tenon shoulder. Locate the table fence so that it is exactly the length of the tenon away from the outer edge of the router cutter; that is, the left hand edge.

Holding the work-piece firmly against the bevel set to cut square, push the bevel forward over the cutter to make a cut to the full depth of the shoulder while scribing the shoulder at the same time. If the diameter of the cutter isn't great enough to cut the full length of the tenon at one pass, move the work piece to the left; again, rest it firmly against the bevel fence and make another pass to remove the waste. Turn the work over and repeat the process. All the tenons can be cut without re-setting if the same depth of shoulder is required.

A cramping pad made from an offcut will prevent the cramps from bruising the rails and also prevent any splintering of the tenon shoulder at the break-through point.

Cutting tenons a different way

If a large number of tenons of the same size have to be cut, it's worth spending time making this small jig which holds each rail against the fence of the router table and allows it to be pushed across the cutter. The exact fit holds the timber securely, and the right hand can be braced against the fence as shown in Fig 252. These photos were taken using the Triton Router Bench, but if the Elu 551 is used, the side cramp can be brought into use at the left hand side of the jig.

251 Tenon jig

252 Pushing the timber through

253 One cheek cut

The housing joint (or dado in the USA)

Perhaps the easiest way of making a bookcase is to use the housing joint, either by placing an open-ended joint at the corner or, to avoid this, by setting the top and bottom shelves a little way back from the front edge of the sides or ends.

The router cannot be used with its own fence, but a strip of timber can be attached using double-sided adhesive tape. This strip should be cut to overlap the timber to provide adequate support for the router at the start and completion of the cut.

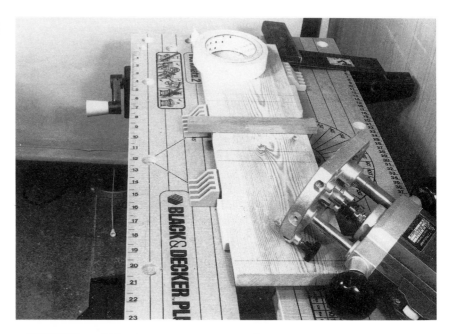

254 The stopped housing – timber held in the Workmate – fence planted on

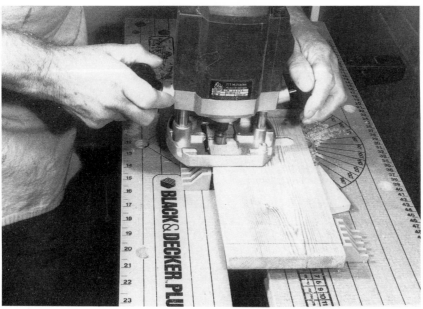

255 The stopped housing – cutting

(right) Table lamp; (overleaf) Wall bookcase and staircase

Measurements will need to be taken for the exact positioning of the strip; if the housing is to be stopped, a stop of some sort must be provided for the router. This can be a simple pencil mark – or perhaps on wide boards a stop-strip can be attached temporarily. The rounded end of the housing can be squared off with a chisel, but many craftsmen prefer to round the edge of the shelf to fit.

When cutting through-housings, in order to prevent splintering or breaking-out when completing each cut, a waste piece should be cramped to the edge of the board.

256 Cutting a housing on the Triton – timber clamped in position

257 Completed housing

In the example shown, the timber is held in the cramping dogs of the Black & Decker Workmate, and a waste piece has been placed underneath the work to clear them.

Another way if a router bench is available and where the router can be used in its normal position, that is, over the work piece, is simplified using the Triton work bench. The router, assembled to the carriage, can be passed across the timber after plunging to the required depth.

I set up a sub-bench top using a piece of blockboard. To this I fixed a stop piece – which also served as a waste block to prevent splintering out at the completion of the cut. A carriage stop, in the shape of a wooden block, was secured to the side slide frame of the bench with a G-cramp. The work was held against the stop with a quick-acting bar cramp since this would lie flat and not interfere in any way with the movement of the carriage.

A line was marked on the stop piece to indicate the centre position of the router, and the timber lined up accurately with this to position each housing perfectly. Once set up, the cutting of the housings is a simple matter and takes a minimum of time. The recessed bookcase was made using this assembly.

Making tongued and grooved board

This material can be quite expensive to buy ready-prepared and generally it has the traditional vee-cut on the tongued edge and a matching groove on the other.

The router, however, offers endless variations – again, depending on the range of cutters available.

The simplest method is to cut the groove, then make two passes with the same router cutter on both faces of the opposite edge to make the tongue. A chamfering cutter can be used to complete the shaping. Alternatively, a beading cutter or similar small shaping cutter can be used to give a more individual touch.

If the boards are fairly wide, a vee-grooving cutter could be run along the centre of each board to enhance the appearance.

Should the job require a quantity of boarding and a router bench is available, its use will speed up the work.

Edge jointing of boards

Wide boards are not only hard to find but rather ex-

pensive; thus the jointing of narrow boards is sometimes the only way.

Perhaps the easiest method is to cut a groove on both edges with the router and insert a tongue made of hardwood pieces sawn across the grain. Alternatively, plywood could be used for the tongue. With thicker boards multiple-tonguing is the answer. Cut the grooves to the exact width of the tonguing pieces which have been cut from plywood. Boards can also be joined using dowels. The plunging router is ideal for this purpose. To minimise warping the boards should be arranged with heart sides alternating.

Cutting an additional rebate in an existing window frame to insert a glass panel for secondary glazing

Where wooden window frames are in good condition, many people fit secondary glazing by adding plastic frames to the inside of the window frame. This can often prove unsightly, and at the same time the seal may not be entirely satisfactory.

To cut a rebate into the existing woodwork using a hammer and chisel can result in broken glass and loss of temper with an accompanying lowering of standards of speech! It is impossible to use the traditional rebate or plough plane in an enclosed frame as they cannot be taken into the corners, and the glass could easily be damaged.

With a router, the job can be simplified and the results very gratifying. First, make an addition to the router fence detailed in Chapter 10, and select a straight panel cutter of width equal to the width of rebate to be cut. Complete the assembly of the router, set the depth gauge, and place the router fence so that the cutter can be fed into the corner of the window (this is only possible with the fence addition). The rebate can, of course, be cut on either the outside or inside of the frame. In either case the glass can be held in place with a small decorative beading – or putty could be used, but only on the outside.

The added fence will rest on the glass and up against the edge of the frame. Push the router carefully into each corner, working from the centre in each case.

Remove hinged frames, and also the hinges and catches, before commencing the cutting. Where there are no casement fasteners or catches the work can be in situ, but be sure there is enough space to use the router safely.

258 *Router fitted with special base to access the corner of a glazed frame*

260 *Final cut into the corner of the frame*

259 *Cutting the new rebate*

Fielded panels

This is a highly skilled job when done by hand, but extremely simple when cut using one of the router sets currently available. Unfortunately, these sets are extremely expensive, and probably out of reach of the pocket of the serious home craftsman. Do not despair, kind reader; the job can be done using only a limited number of router cutters.

The panel should be prepared to fit the door frame but should be slightly undersize all round by about 3mm to take up any movement of the timber. This type of panel is never glued.

Insert a straight router cutter in the router collet, and assemble the fence to cut a groove at the required distance from the edge to form a raised step. Carefully cut a groove all round.

Decrease the distance from the fence to the cutter by the diameter of the cutter and take another pass all round. Do this successively until all the waste has been removed. The slope can be worked with a bench plane, and final touching up with a shoulder plane. Shaping of the raised edge of the panel can be attained by using a suitable router cutter.

Panels can also be raised and further enhanced with the addition of a cocked bead. Cut the groove to receive the bead with a straight cutter. The bead strip can be cut using the tunnel system shown on page 56, or a strip can be cut on the edge of a board by making two cuts, one from each side, with an ovolo bit to form the cocked bead. The edge should then be sliced off with the circular saw.

Another method of cutting the groove to receive the cocked bead is to use a frame of wooden strips to act as a guide. Add a sub-base to the router (in this case the Elu 177E); the sub-base runs on the edge of the frame and keeps the router at an exact distance while the groove is being cut. The sub-base can, of course, be used for any number of similar applications.

There are a number of instances where the router will be needed to cut without the support of the actual timber – in the case of a carving to remove the ground, or possibly on narrow timber where the use of a fence is impossible. In the photograph the work piece is held in the Workmate 2, and the bench top itself is used to support an attachment added to the

261 Frame guide in use

262 Ski attachment

fence arms and called a 'ski'. This allows the router to be moved over the work at a fixed depth, permits the removal of the waste, and the accurate planing of the surface.

Another application of the ski is in the planing of the rough end of a block of timber prior to mounting it in the lathe. A frame on which the ski can slide must first be made to surround the block. If this idea were to be adopted by a woodturner, a box framework into which the block could be fixed could be used over and over again.

An aid to cutting mortises is the addition of another fence. The fences are set equidistantly so that the router cutter, of exactly the same size as the required mortise, cuts in the centre of the pieces to be mortised. This requires accurate preparation of the timber, prevents any rocking of the router, and ensures perfectly square-cut mortises.

Offset mortises can be cut using the same set-up.

Edging of table and stool tops is simplified using the router either by hand with the fence fitted, or if the top is shaped, by either using the curved fence or router cutters with guide pins, or by using the better self-guide bearing type. If a router table is available, then this type of cutting can be greatly simplified.

Chamfer, ovolo, rounding-over, and other similar cutters, can be used to marked effect.

Take care when using the cutters which have guide pins; move the router as quickly as possible along the edge to avoid any possibility of scorching – with the high speed of the router cutter this is always possible.

Butt hinge fitting

This template is described on page 79. The one used was designed to receive a 102mm (4in) steel butt hinge. I always write the size of the cutter and guide bush on each template.

Fit both the guide bush and the straight cutter to the router. Position and secure the template either with a G-cramp – my example was held with a G-cramp, with the whole assembly held in the vice, but a job carried out on site will necessitate using double-sided adhesive tape. Plunge and rout out the waste. It's a very quick little trick!

The router used as a lining-out tool

When fitted with a small vee cutter, or similar, the router makes an excellent job of lining out a carving – both three-dimensional and in relief.

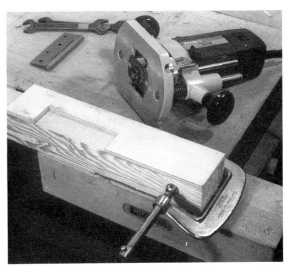

263 Hinge template secured to door-frame upright

264 Testing for hinge fit

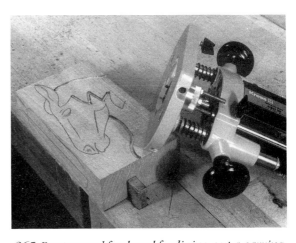

265 Router used freehand for lining-out a carving

266 *Angled cuts with a timber guide planted-on*

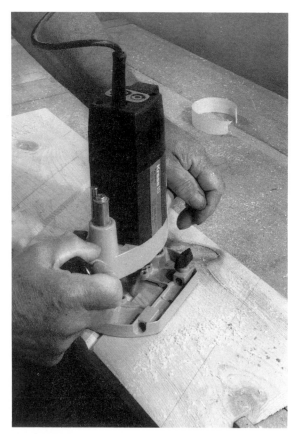

267 *Straight side of the router base runs against the guide*

Fence – planted-on

Many situations will arise where standard fences cannot be used, and the craftsman must then solve the problem by adding a fence. The cut may be straight or curved, and a strip of timber can be cut and attached to the work piece – using double-sided adhesive tape to act as a guide.

If the cut is made completely across a board, it is wise to make the fence to overlap in order to give support at the start and completion of the cut. In the case of straight cuts, the edge of the router can run against the planted-on fence. If a curved cut is to be made, the curvature of the router base may permit its use as a guide; otherwise a guide bush must be fitted to the router base.

CUTTING THROUGH DOVETAILS WITH THE LEIGH DOVETAIL JIG

Cutting the sockets

a Place the work piece in the vertical cramp and check for squareness.

b Use the through-dovetail pin-mode to set the dovetail spacing.

c Move the finger guide to the tail scale and set it at ALL.

d Select the cutter and guide bush to suit the thickness of timber to be used: see table, page 165.

e Set the dovetail cutter depth to that of the pin board thickness and allow a little extra for cleaning up.

f Rout out the waste between the finger guides, always working from left to right, to cut all the sockets; Fig 268A.

Cutting the pins

a Flip over the finger assembly to the through-dovetails pin-mode and set the scale to the diameter of the dovetail cutter; Fig 268B.

b Place the work piece in the vertical clamp.

c Select the appropriate straight cutter and guide bush to suit.

d Set the depth of cut of the straight cutter to that of the tail board thickness plus a little extra for cleaning up.

e With the router, remove the waste between the finger guides to create the pins; Fig 268C.

268 a Leigh jig – through-dovetail – tail pieces

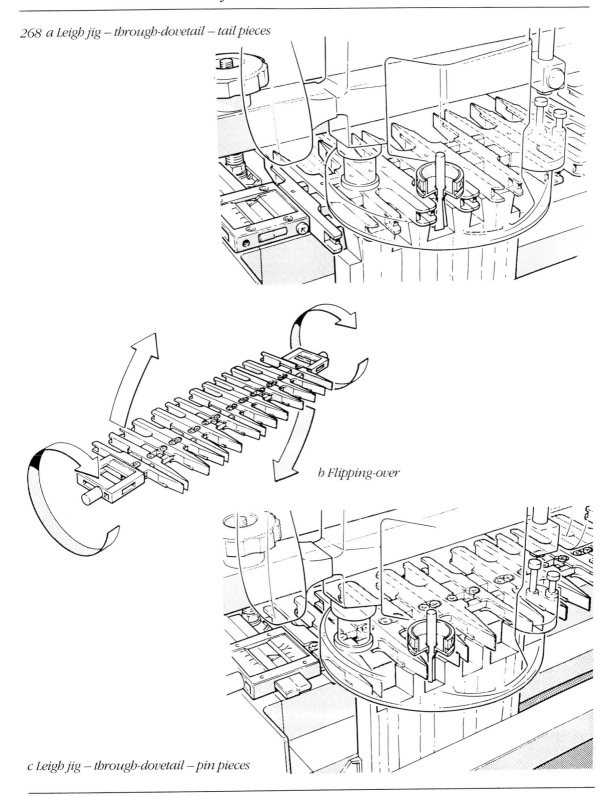

b Flipping-over

c Leigh jig – through-dovetail – pin pieces

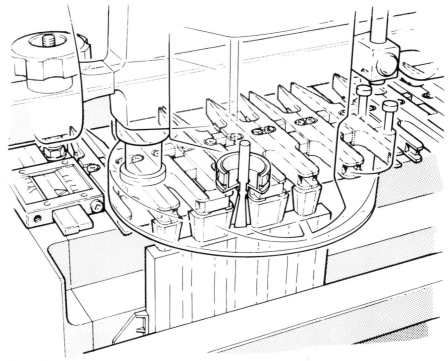

269 a Leigh dovetail jig – half-lap dovetails – tail pieces

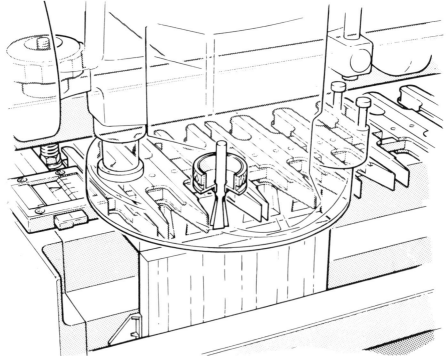

b Leigh dovetail jig – half-lap dovetail – pin pieces

It is suggested that trial joints be cut before using the jig on cabinet construction in order to establish a system of adjustment in the case of badly fitting joints. This is not a difficult matter, but an understanding of the system is necessary. If a test-fit is made between the two components, should the joint be loose, the finger assembly must be moved out slightly; if tight, the finger assembly must be move in.

Lapped dovetails (known as 'half-blind' in the USA)

Cutting the tails

a It is suggested that the user cuts a spacer board when cutting the lap dovetail and places it between the finger assembly and the jig body, and under the rear clamp bar. The board provides a flush surface upon which the finger assembly will sit comfortably, and also acts as a backing board which will prevent the possibility of the wood tearing out.

b Set the finger assembly to the HB Mode (as marked on the jig) and set the scale to the thickness of the material used for the sockets.

c Place the work carefully in the front vertical clamp and check for squareness.

d Set up the fingers to suit the job.

e Make and install bridge pieces between the rounded finger ends.

f Select the correct size of dovetail cutter and guide bush.

g Adjust the depth of cut of the dovetail cutter.

h Cut the waste between the fingers.

Cutting the pins

a Do not change either the finger setting or the depth of cut.

b Flip over the finger assembly to the HB pin side and set the scale to the thickness of the tail pieces.

c Fit the work piece in the jig and check for accuracy of setting.

d Rout out the pins.

It is again suggested that test pieces be made and a system be devised for the fine fitting of the joint components. Make the test piece, and try it for fit. Adjust the finger assembly in for deeper sockets and out for shallower ones. Make a special note of the details for future use.

Using the jig becomes a simple matter after reading the manual supplied with it. The detail given may give the impression of great complication, but this isn't so; the makers are just keen to give the user a complete picture of the versatility of the tool. Certainly no production workshop should be without one of these, and the serious home craftsman will find great joy in using it.

PIN PIECE THICKNESS	DOVETAIL CUTTER	STRAIGHT CUTTER CUTTER DIA. x DEPTH	GUIDE BUSH OUTSIDE DIA.	MAX. TAIL THICKNESS	CLOSEST PIN CENTERS
FROM 1/4" TO 1/2"	#70 (3/8 x 8° x 1/2)	5/16" x 1"	7/16"	1"	1"
FROM 1/2" TO 13/16"	#80 (1/2 x 8° x 13/16)	5/16" x 1"	7/16"	1"	1"
FROM 3/4" TO 1"	#90 (11/16 x 8° x 1)	1/2 x 1"	5/8"	1"	1–3/16"
FROM 7/8" TO 1–1/4 "	#100 (13/16 x 8° x 1–1/4)	7/16 x 1"	5/8"	1"	1–1/4"

16 The Router on the Lathe

A woodturning buff like myself would be expected to explore the possibility of using the lathe and router together. Some years back, I read an article in one of the woodworking magazines which described how the writer had used the router in a frame mounted over the lathe headstock. I made such a frame, but have never used it since I moved to this delightful part of the world and found other things to do. However, I have found the frame but cannot find the article, since I tend to give my magazines away after a while. The framework was originally designed around the Myford Lathe which I had then; thus, it's a re-design to suit the Graduate.

The project is to use the router to shape and mould (if you like), the side, or edge, or inside of a previously turned bowl to give it a completely new look. This is done by mounting the router on a cradle which can be swung over, or into, the bowl. The cradle can be set at any height in relation to the bowl since its sides are bored with a series of holes at the centre – which, in turn, match similar holes in the frame which is attached to the lathe bed. The frame can be set at any distance from the headstock to suit the requirements of the design and the size of the work.

If routing is to be done at equidistant stages around the periphery of the bowl, some method of setting and locking the measurements must be arrived at. When I first had the Graduate lathe, it had with it an enormous faceplate made in aluminium – indeed a useless piece of equipment. I marked this up and bored holes accurately, and used it as a dividing head, fitting it to the left hand end of the lathe. Craft Supplies have one in smaller form to suit most lathes – or one could be made in timber and attached to a small faceplate. For those turners who possess a Multistar chuck, the whole business is simplified since the body of this chuck is bored around its periphery with 24 equidistant holes and the makers supply an arm with a locking pin which can be attached to the lathe. This is seen in Fig 270.

The bowl blank, which was in sycamore, was at-tached to the chuck and turned completely to the finished stage; then it was sealed with a coat of sanding sealer. If you are doing this routing for the first time, leave the bowl with a wall just a little thicker than normal to avoid accidents.

Whichever method you use to hold the bowl during turning, stick to it to begin your routing. Later, when experience comes, the type of cut and its size can be accurately worked out; but until you explore the possibilities you cannot be quite sure of what you are going to get.

270 Multistar chuck – indexing attachment

271 Multistar chuck with turned bowl – indexing pin centre left

273 Cutter plunged to make the first cut

272 Router and cradle located in the main frame

274 Cutting proceeds

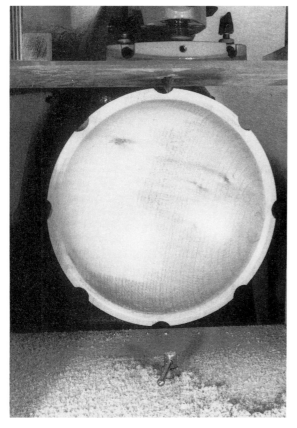

275 Last swing

276 Second cuts progressing

277 Completed bowl

Choose a simple cutter to start with; a round one with a simple rounding-over type curve will suit. Set the router up, adjust and fix the depth of cut, locking the router cutter in the cutting position. Secure the dividing-head device locking pin (or swing the locking pin arm into position in the case of the Multistar chuck). Switch on the router; and gently, at first, swing the cradle so that the router cutter moves from the rim of the bowl down the outside. Not too slowly – otherwise frictional burning will take place. Have a look to see the result after switching off – it's surprising how good this first look is! Take out the locking pin, and move over to the next selected division hole. Take another cut, and do this progressively until all the proposed cuts have been made. In the example shown in Fig 277, two different settings of the cradle were made to give two sizes of tapered flutes; the results you can see.

The router can be set inside, or on top, of the cradle, and the latter can be swung from both sides of the headstock. Cutting can also be carried out inside the bowl by fixing the carriage and using the plunge mechanism of the router to bring on the cut.

After all the cuts have been made, the frame can be removed, and any touching up with abrasive paper can be done. If the router cutter was in first class condition, little will need to be done although some scorching may have to be removed from those first few cuts. Apply polish to each flute in turn; then put a final coat or two on the completed bowl. If a liquid polish is used, take great care; apply it sparingly with the lathe stopped, and cut it back with steel wool. Overloading would result in 'tear-drop' runs into the flutes which would take a great deal of effort to remove.

This type of routing can be a fun thing. Experiment with boxes, vases, and spindled work of all kinds and surprise yourself!

Router used on work turned between centres

The router can be used to shape and make decorative cuts on work turned between centres such as table, chair and stool legs, standard lamps, table lamps, newel posts, and similar articles.

The basic requirement is a track along which the router can be moved between the headstock and tailstock. The one illustrated was made from 51mm x 51mm (2in by 2in) deal supported by two end frames made of multi-plywood. The frame at the headstock end must be shaped to clear the work, and the tailstock must be unobstructed at the opposite end. The frame is attached to a baseboard, which in turn is fixed to the lathe bed using G-cramps. The router must be a snug fit in the track, and the latter should be waxed to give easy movement.

If cuts are to be made equidistantly around the turned work, a method of sub-dividing and holding the setting must be devised. In the example shown in Fig 279, the Multistar chuck is again in use – this time,

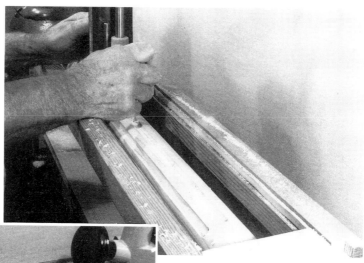

278 Fluting a table leg

279 Router approaching the stop

fitted with an adapter which accepts the No2 Morse taper driving fork used in the lathe headstock; see Fig 271 for details. When all the settings have been made, the router is placed at the start position at the tailstock end; then plunged to full depth and moved along the track. A quick, easy movement will give perfect cutting.

Any number of variations of cut can be made. Many will want to try using the router as the turning tool, running both lathe and router at the same time. This is certainly possible, but personally I prefer to turn my shapes by hand. The Sears Router Crafter offers this type of facility; but, in addition, the timber can be turned slowly by hand to facilitate the making of spiral cuts.

Further headstock work

A track similar to the one used for work between centres, but in this case arranged to pass the router across the headstock, can be used to add many features to a piece of turnery. Once again, the dividing head system is needed if settings are to be made and held while the routing is taking place. No problems should occur here, but do keep the router cutters very sharp to produce first class cutting which will require very little abrasive work on completion.

Woodlathe dividing head

A reference to this attachment was made on page 166. It comprises a simple faceplate which has twelve equally spaced holes drilled around its periphery, and is fitted over the lathe shaft and clamped into position on to the faceplate or chuck. A locating pin and bracket are provided for fitting to the lathe. Five sizes of centre hole are available to suit the most common lathe shaft sizes: 19mm, 25mm, 29mm, and 38mm (¾in, 1in, 1⅛in, and 1½in).

281 Faceplate converted to a dividing head

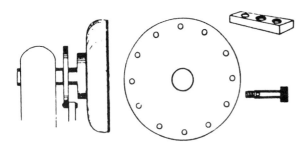

280 Woodlathe dividing head

282 Large faceplate converted to a dividing head – spring-loaded plunger for locking

A number of manufacturers offer the dividing head as an optional extra, the one made by Williams and Hussey in the USA is an excellent example. If the reader has one of the very large faceplates supplied as standard by several manufacturers he may care to make his own. The one seen in Figs 281 and 282 was made by the author from the faceplate supplied with his Graduate lathe.

Bowl-blanks: preparation for mounting on a precision combination chuck

Bowl-blanks are usually held for first turning on a faceplate, a pin chuck, or a chuck ring; but cutting a dovetail recess in the bowl blank itself eliminates the need for anything except the combination chuck.

The precision combination chuck has an expanding collet which, when the chuck collar is turned, slides into a recess cut in the timber. This recess is undercut in dovetail form to locate on to the sloping edged jaws of the chuck collet.

A template has to be made for use in conjunction with a guide bush and dovetail router cutter. Make the necessary calculations (see page 99) and mark out a circle on a piece of multi-plywood of suitable thickness. The recess can be cut using the router freehand with a straight cutter. For this particular application, I usually make my templates circular to ensure centrality when locating them on the work piece.

With the template completed, secure the block and attach the template to it with double-sided adhesive tape. Place the dovetail cutter in the collet, and screw the guide bush in place. Set the depth to the thickness of the plywood plus 8mm (5/16in). Switch on the router and plunge the dovetail cutter, which will cut as it descends. The moment it reaches full depth, move it carefully around the template, being guided by the bush.

Remove and test. I have three of these and find them great time savers.

283 Preparation of bowl – turning blanks to receive the precision combination chuck

284 Fitting the chuck

Projects

Sycamore wall clock and bowl

Small Teak Stand

285 Small stand

Cutting list for stand (finished sizes)						
	L	W	T	L	W	T
		mm			inches	
1 piece teak	229	251	29	9	9⅞	1⅛

This is a simple first exercise to introduce freehand cutting, using an ovolo cutter with a guide pin.

One difficulty which often arises with the beginner (and I must confess that I often feel very much a beginner), is how best to judge the rate of feed of the router across the work. Slow speed often results in burning of the cut edge; too fast a speed can overload the machine or result in poor control, which with the router cutter and guide pin can result in inaccurate work. Using the router freehand is one of the best ways to familiarise yourself with the effects produced by different speeds and patterns

The work piece can be held on the bench top using double-sided adhesive tape. Make sure that the work and the bench are free from dust before attaching the tape. Arrange the timber so that it slightly overlaps the edge of the bench; the timber should, of course, have been cut and planed to the exact size required.

286 Small stand in teak – double-sided tape used for holding

287 Cutting an ovolo

Be sure that the router base is level with the bench top, and make the first cuts with the grain. At the commencement of the cut, hold the router firmly with slight inward pressure against the edge to ensure a perfect start. As the end of the work piece is approached, release the side pressure slightly to avoid running the cutter around the corner. Make the cuts across the grain when both long grain cuts are completed.

If the completed stand is to be used in the kitchen, it can be finished using a cooking oil. Elsewhere, the finish will depend on the use to which it is to be put.

Small Stand with Tile Insert

288 *Small stand with tile inserted*

Cutting list for small stand with tile insert (finished sizes)							
	L	W	T		L	W	T
		mm				inches	
1 piece teak (or similar wood)	203	226	29		8	8⅞	1⅛

This can be used as a tea or coffee pot stand or as a stand for a plant pot. This one is made of teak and is in use as a teapot stand. It is intended as a first-step project just to introduce the router.

Prepare the timber by planing it to size and sawing it to length; choose an uncomplicated outer shape – indeed, it can be left as a square or rectangle.

Mark it out and secure it to the bench top with two strips of double-sided adhesive tape. Be sure to dust down the surface of the bench and the timber before attaching the tape, and choose a smooth flat area. Insert a 12.7 (½in) panel cutter into the collet of the router, and close the collet with the spanners.

It is suggested that for this first exercise and, bearing in mind that the final depth is to be 16mm (⅝in), that the cutting be done in two stages. Set the fence to 19mm (¾in) from the outside of the cutter, and

adjust the depth stop to 8mm (⁵⁄₁₆in). Tighten down firmly on all screws.

Remember to keep the fence up tight to the edge of the work piece; switch on the machine, and plunge into one of the corners. The moment you are at full depth move the router along fairly quickly and certainly instantaneously to avoid burning the timber, as slow movement will tend to leave scorch marks. If you move too fast, the router will labour and you will know on the instant. Stop at the corner – you may have to peer over the machine to get a good sighting. Change direction from this point and proceed to cut the next side, then follow through with the remaining two sides.

Remove the router, switch off and set the depth gauge to 16mm (⅝in). Repeat the cutting of the sides to full depth. Switch off once again and remove

289 Recess routed

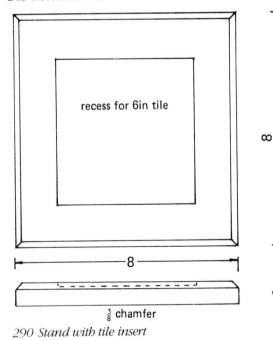

recess for 6in tile

8

8

$\frac{7}{8}$

$\frac{3}{8}$ chamfer

290 Stand with tile insert

the fence. Set the depth to 8mm ($\frac{5}{16}$in) once more. Using the router freehand remove the central waste, work carefully at first but do it methodically – running from side to side and keeping the cutter away from the already perfect sides. When these first passes have been made, repeat them to remove the remainder. This should give you great confidence and help to build up a procedure for safety in your mind.

Clean up the piece as necessary, insert the tile, securing it with Evostick or similar impact glue.

If the edge is to be decorated with a simple finish, do it after the tile housing has been cut, as follows: remove the panel cutter and insert a chamfering cutter; setting it to remove a very small chamfer. Set the fence. Place the stand in the vice and proceed to cut a chamfer on each edge. It will be found advisable to have a piece of waste wood at the end of the edge to avoid any splintering. It also helps to cut the two long grain edges first, as this reduces the chance of splintering. Finish as before; if you are fortunate to have a piece of teak just give it an oil finish – Mazola oil will be fine but it will darken the timber a little.

Freehand Caricature

291 Drawing of caricature

Cutting list for caricature (finished sizes)						
	L	W	T	L	W	T
		mm			inches	
1 piece of any suitable close grained hardwood	305	229	16	12	9	⅝

292 Routing a caricature – drawing transferred to the timber

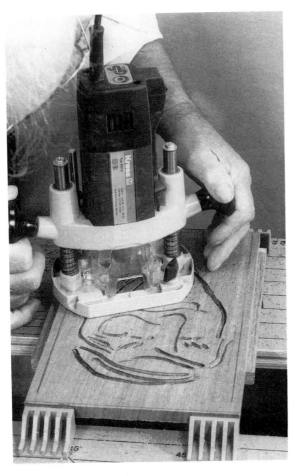

293 Caricature-routing

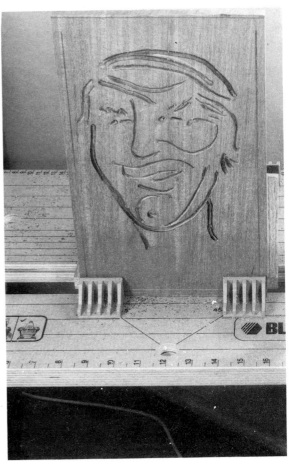

294 Caricature completed

This can be made up into a small plaque for wall hanging, but the main purpose is to provide freehand work with the discipline of having to accurately follow a line, and to gradually withdraw the cutter at the end of each cut to run out to a point.

Prepare a board of fairly close grain – not too well figured, otherwise the grain will detract from the cut design and reduce the visual impact. Finish the face as for polishing.

With the router disconnected, remove the fence, and insert a veining cutter of a size to suit the desired width of cut. Set the depth stop to 3mm (1/8in). Make sure everything is tightened down before plugging in the router and switching it on. Once again, it is important to be able to see the tip of the cutter as it cuts so that the line can be accurately followed. If you

have a dust extraction system use it to clear the chips away from the point of cut.

Secure the work piece using double-sided tape or on the Workmate, switch on, and plunge the router at any convenient point of start. Move as quickly as accuracy and safety will permit, and as the end of a particular cut is made, slowly release the plunge so that the width of the cut reduces to a point at full withdrawal. Most of the cuts will be like this in the design I have shown here, although some will end at full depth. Take your time; with so little depth to be cut, speed of feed is not quite so vital.

After completion clean up the surface if necessary. Brush in a coat of Briwax, leave for a few minutes then polish with a lint-free cloth.

Carved Number Plate

295 Completed number plate

Cutting list for house name board (finished sizes)						
	L	W	T	L	W	T
		mm			inches	
1 piece hardwood suitable for exterior use	381	178	22	15	7	7/8
Recommended timbers, all to be straightgrained: elm, iroko, oak, teak, Western Red cedar.						

For a project of this kind the router can be used freehand or in conjunction with lettering templates or stencils; see page 92. Unfortunately, these usually offer only a limited range of styles, and many craftsmen will opt to select their own, and will therefore have to refer to a book on typography. For this first adventure into name or number boards, it is suggested that the style selected is made up of straight lines wherever possible.

I've chosen to carve the letter 'one' and selected a piece of teak which is fairly close grained and without knots; timber of very marked grain will tend to distract the eye. Plan the lettering using graph paper or mark out using squares and check for good proportion; I always refer to the Roman Alphabet for this. Transfer the lettering to the board which should have been accurately planed and cut to exact length, particularly if we are to add some edge decoration.

We shall need a 3mm (1/8in) cutter for marking out and for making the border cut; a 12.7mm (1/2in) cutter for removing the groundwork; and a 12.7mm (1/2in) rounding-over cutter with a guide pin for the edge treatment.

After inserting the 3mm (1/8in) panel cutter, place the fence in position 19mm (3/4in) away from the cutter. Set the depth gauge to 10mm (3/8in). Check everything for security and hold down the timber by one of the methods suggested in Chapter 8; always place the timber close to the edge of the bench to make access easier.

Holding the fence firmly against the edge of the timber, rout a groove all round the face to set up a border, taking care as you approach the end of each pass. Switch off, and set the fence to 32mm (1 1/4in). Rout once again along each side – this will determine the limits for the lettering. By changing the

296 House number plate – marking out using squares

fence settings almost all the lines can be routed, leaving only the minimum of waste to be removed freehand. Switch off and remove the fence; then switch on and carefully cut each letter, following the lines. Switch off, remove the cutter and insert the 12.7mm (½in) panel cutter. Now switch on, and carefully remove the remainder of the waste, and touch up as necessary.

297 First rout to define the border

Insert the rounding-over cutter after re-setting the depth gauge to 12.7mm (½in). Plunge the router before commencing the cut and move along the edge quite quickly – insufficient speed may cause the guide pin to burn the timber by excessive friction. Once again take care when approaching the end of each run.

With a little touch-up with abrasive paper the job will now be complete. A suitable finish should be applied depending on the position of the job and the type of weather conditions it is likely to be subjected to.

Incised Lettering

298 Incised lettering

Cutting list for board with incised lettering (finished sizes)						
	L	W mm	T	L	W inches	T
1 piece closegrained hardwood of your choice	457	152	19	18	6	¾

Once confidence is built up, an approach to incised lettering can be considered. A choice of style can be made, and many will opt for script. A number of different shapes of cut, or profile, may suggest themselves, but for this exercise I have chosen a vee-cutter.

As always the lettering should be marked out most carefully and this can be done by transferring it from a paper pattern or marking it directly on the timber, which should have been planed and cut to size. Remove the fence on the router, set the depth gauge to 6mm (¼in) or a suitable depth, depending on the size of the job and the degree of prominence needed for this particular project.

We shall need to see the point of the cutter at all times to ensure accuracy. Try to regard the router as a large pen (a noisy one perhaps, but efficient and it doesn't smudge!), plunge the cutter and carefully move forward along the line. If the cutter has to be lifted and removed, do so by gently and gradually releasing the plunge so that the cut ends at a point. A flow is quickly attained and the final result has to be admired.

For the diffident ones it may be best to make some practice runs on pieces of scrap. These should be made completely freehand without lines at first, then with lines until the technique is mastered. Following the lines may be a little difficult, but possibly the smooth release of the plunge may be more troublesome. Apply a finish to suit.

Kitchen Wall Clock

299 *Kitchen wall clock*
with tile insert

Cutting list for kitchen wall clock (finished sizes)						
	L	W	T	L	W	T
		mm			inches	
1 piece sycamore	305	229	32	12	9	1¼

Also required: one 152mm (6in) square tile; one clock unit with hands.

This project uses a 152mm (6in) square tile suitable for a kitchen clock. These tiles come in many designs and can be fixed in place with a contact adhesive.

Prepare a block of suitable hardwood by planing and sawing to size; I used sycamore. Mark up both faces with outlines of the recesses to be cut for the tile and for the battery-powered clock unit. Having fixed the block to the bench top securely, choose a straight router cutter and fix it firmly in the collet. Set the depth gauge to the thickness of the tile, and arrange the fence so that the cutter will make a first cut fractionally inside the limit line for the tile recess. Switch on and plunge to full depth, cutting each inside edge in turn. The fence can still be re-set to make the inside cuts to remove the remainder of the waste, but the reader may care to make this an exercise in freehand routing. When complete, make a skim cut along the edge to bring the recess to exactly six inches and to perfect the finish. The round corners will have to be squared up with a mortise chisel.

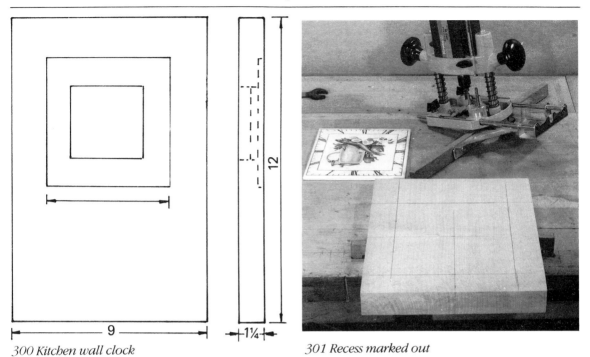

12

9

1¼

300 Kitchen wall clock

301 Recess marked out

302 First cut using the fence

303 Fence cuts completed

304 Recess routed freehand and tile checked for fit

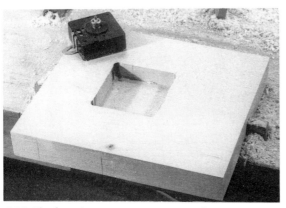

305 Clock unit recess cut on reverse face

The outer edges of the block can be completed by working them with an ovolo or other decorative cutter.

Reverse the block, set the depth gauge to half the required depth, set up the fence and rout out the clock body recess. Take a second cut to come to the full depth – two cuts will avoid motor overload and save wear or even breakage of the cutter.

If a keyhole cutter is available use this in the router to cut a screwhead recess for hanging. If one isn't, then a small brass keyhole escutcheon can be used, the recess being made with a cutter of suitable size to give sufficient clearance for the screwhead. Clean up with abrasive paper and apply a suitable polish.

Patio Fencing

Cutting list for patio fencing (finished sizes)						
	L	W	T	L	W	T
		mm			inches	
Softwood slats, each	610	127	19	24	5	¾
Posts and rails to your choice.						

This is one of the many projects which can be tackled using the hinged box type template. The fence should be made of an available softwood; the one I have is in 127mm by 19mm (5in by ¾in) slats, each 610mm (24in) long.

Draw out the design for the cut-out which will entail working with a guide bush attached to the base of the router. Choose a cutter which must be of the piercing and side cutting type, plus a suitably-sized guide bush; calculate the allowance to be made in cutting the template, see page 99 for details. Mark out the template on to a piece of hardboard, and cut out the design with the router. This template will be hinged to the box, see page 81. Narrow strips of rubber tacked on the underside of the template should provide enough adhesion to hold the work piece firmly, but if there is any difficulty, double-sided adhesive tape could be used.

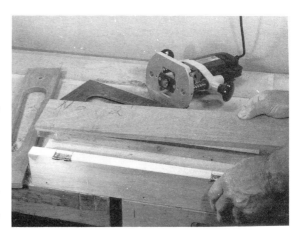

306 Patio fencing – inserting the prepared timber into the template box

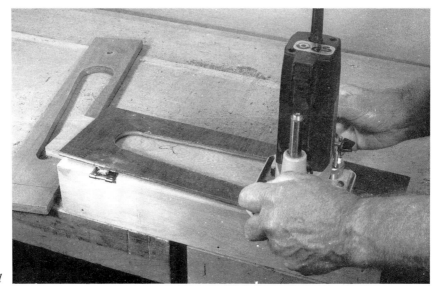

307 Routing commenced

308 Routing completed

Secure the box in the vice, place the first strip of fencing in position after placing a positioning mark on each strip. Insert the cutter into the router which has been already fitted with the guide bush. Plug in, switch on, and carefully plunge right through the strip; now move forward in a clockwise direction, allowing the guide to follow the curves. Don't move too quickly or undue strain on the cutter might result in breakage. Carry out the same procedure with all the strips.

A nice capping, finished with a rounding-over cutter, will add a touch of class to the job.

Table Lamp

Cutting list for table lamp (finished sizes)	L	W	T		L	W	T
		mm				inches	
2 pieces mahogany or similar	254	178	16		10	7	5/8
2 pieces mahogany or similar	254	172	16		10	6¾	5/8
1 piece mahogany or similar	172	172	16		6¾	6¾	5/8

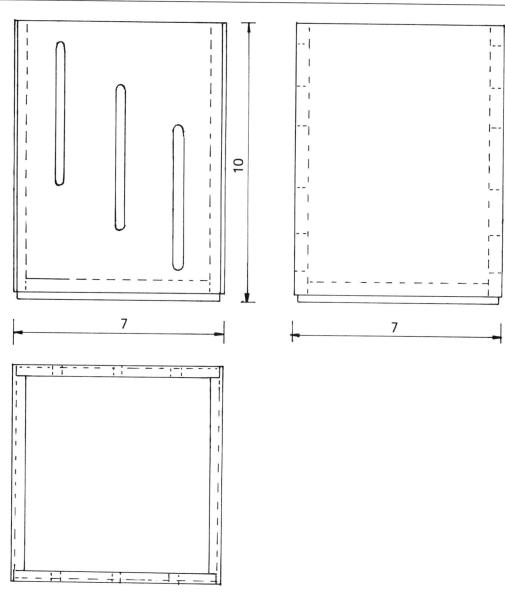

309 Alternative method using pegboard jig – commencing a cut – peg at the point of start

The design incorporates five pieces of timber; four to make up a box form and the fifth to provide a base. It is designed to allow light to pass through the open top and also through the slotted sides. Thin mahogany was chosen. Some thirty years old, it seemed suitable by reason of age – since heat may tend seriously to warp new timber.

The sides are housed into each other, using a rebate cut to the full thickness of the timber. The base is also rebated to its full thickness so that it can be inserted from underneath. The job can be made completely on the router bench; but it's a simple job to cut the housings on the woodwork bench, and to make the slots in the same way as on the router table, but using the router fence and stop marks on the timber itself.

Alternatively, a jig can be made to house each piece, with pegboard used at each end to hold plastic

310 Completing the cut – peg acting as a stop

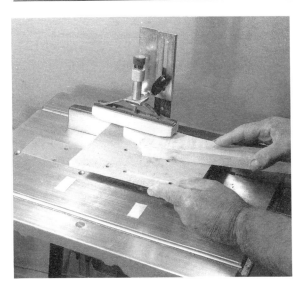

311 Table lamp – side bored and held above the cutter – push stick at the ready

or wooden pegs which act as 'stops' and 'starts' for the router, thus limiting the length of each slot. If the job is done on the router table, suitable start and stop marks must be clearly made to position the timber for the start of the cut and to act as a length indicator. I use masking tape, which can be clearly seen. Using a push stick on top of the flat board, and with a pierce-and-side cutting bit in the router, the timber is pressed on to the cutter, and gently lowered by pressure through the push stick, which is then used to push the timber through to the point of stop. This may seem a little difficult, but using the push stick like this makes it easy. Do all four panels in the same way.

The job must be glued and pinned together before cleaning up. A hard finish using Danish Oil will be found highly suitable.

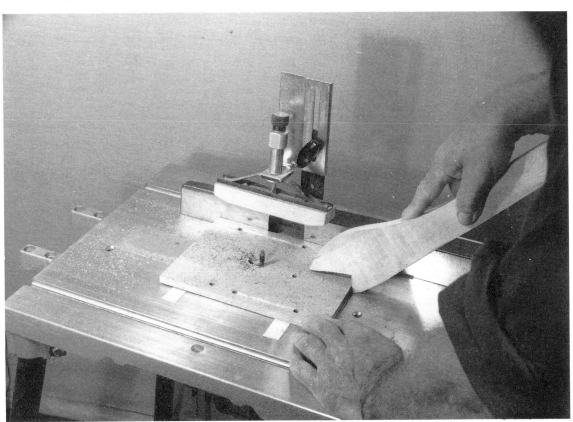

312 Cutting a slot

Small Stool

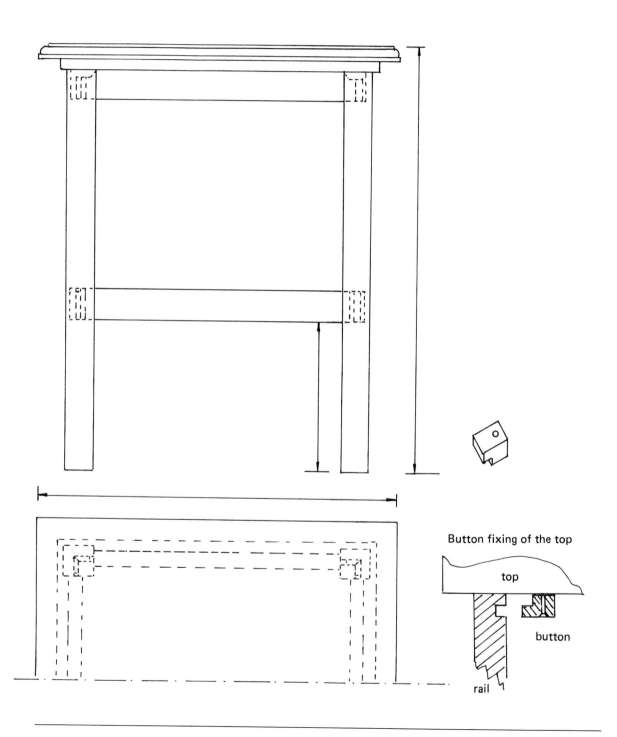

Button fixing of the top

top

button

rail

Cutting list for small stool (finished sizes)	L	W	T		L	W	T
		mm				inches	
A good quality hardwood: 1 top	380	380	22		15	15	7/8
4 legs	305	25	25		12	1	1
8 rails	305	25	25		12	1	1

Rail thickness could be reduced to 22mm (7/8in) to save on costs.

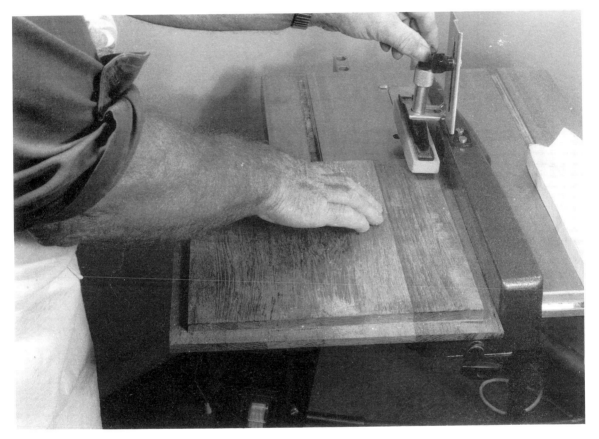

313 Small stool – rebate cut around the underside – cutting the ovolo around the top edge

This is a design for a small stool in teak to match the occasional table; it was made entirely from re-claimed timber.

It uses the sloping haunch mortise and tenon joint for the top rails, and stub tenons, (known as 'blind' in the USA), mitred inside, for the lower rails. Choose one of the methods of making the parts of the joints detailed in Chapter 15.

This particular top was made from 51mm by 25mm (2in by 1in) teak strips, glued together by rubbed jointing; but as this is a complicated process they

314 Completed top

could be tongued and grooved with the router. Once the glue has set, the top is planed to thickness and squared up. Since the top would look rather heavy for the slim legs and rails, a rebate can be cut 19mm (¾in) wide by 10mm (⅜in) deep around the underside.

For edge decoration you can use a small Roman ogee cutter. Both the rebate and the ogee were cut using the Elu 551 router bench. Several different methods can be used for holding the top to the framing, and in this case small screw-blocks made on the router were used. On larger pieces these are called 'buttons' and have tongues which slide in grooves cut on the inside of the rails; in this design they were planted on.

315 Finished stool

Wall Bookcase

This design was made using the Triton Workbench which is rapidly becoming a firm friend of many of my pupils.

The material used was deal, 228mm by 22mm (9in by 7⁄8in) nominal. It was already PAR (planed all round), and bought from a local stockist. Simple location marks were placed on the timber to indicate the position of the shelves after the sides had been cut to exact length.

Arrange the router on the slide chassis of the optional router set-up, removing the saw chassis in order to provide a stop for the material. I made a small stand to locate under the bookcase sides, and this also raised the pieces and saved raising the lower table. A small block was placed at a point on the slide rail so that it could act as a stop to limit the travel of the router, stopping the housing at a point 25mm (1in) away from the edge of the board.

Use G-cramps and cramping pads to secure the timber after locating it exactly in relation to the cutter. If the cutter is not wide enough to make the housing in one pass, two passes will need to be made. Set the router depth gauge to give a 10mm (3⁄8in) cut.

When every check has been made, plug the router into the isolator socket on the Triton after locking the router in the 'on' position. Switch on at the bench switch and plunge the router, pushing the carrier easily across its slides – the simplicity of this has to be experienced. The carrier will finally come to rest against the stop, when you can switch off by using your knee against the stop panel on the front of the Workbench. For wider housings the timber will need to be moved and another pass taken. Cut all the housings in this way, including the open housing at the top.

Each shelf can be notched by hand at the front, or cut on the bandsaw. This design didn't require a back, but if one is needed the rebate can be easily cut with the router, using a panel router cutter. A small plinth can be fitted at the base to lift the lower shelf.

The job was finally glued up, pushed into the recess and painted.

316 Wall bookcase

Sycamore Wall Clock

Cutting list for wall clock (finished sizes)						
	L	W	T	L	W	T
		mm			inches	
1 piece any suitable hardwood (eg sycamore)	305	203	38	12	8	1½

Also required: one clock unit with hands.

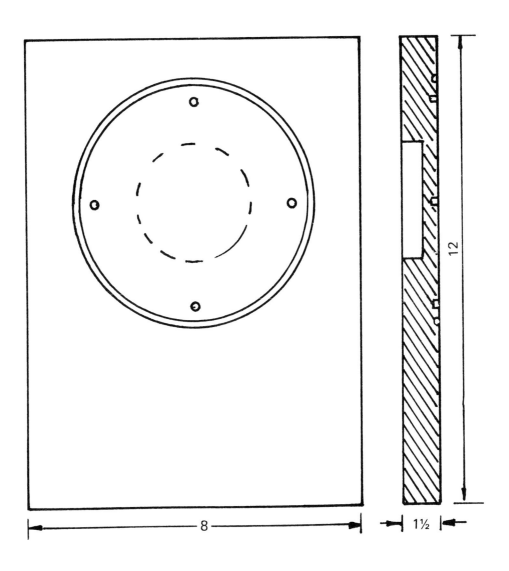

After initial preparation of the wood, the clock can be made using the router only. The outline of the face is cut, using a 12.7mm (½in) corebox cutter. The router must have the maker's trammel bar fitted; alternatively, the reader may care to make one from Perspex like the one shown in use here and detailed on page 80. I confess to a marked reluctance to use any other as this gives me complete control.

Carefully mark the centre for the trammel point on the timber; set the depth gauge on the router and carefully plunge, and immediately move, the router around the job – taking care to hold down firmly all the time while moving forward. Be sure that the cable doesn't wrap around the router, which could not only obstruct the view of the cutter, but also create a dangerous situation. Several passes can be taken and a fairly quick movement will avoid scoring. A cable holder as shown on page 23 will be helpful.

When the face is completed turn the work piece over, and hold it between bench dogs to enable the recess for the clock unit to be cut. In this, I have deliberately chosen to make the cut using the router with a bush guide fitted and a circular template attached to the timber with double-sided tape. Several plunges will need to be taken to reach the required depth. The centre ground can then be removed, again with fairly shallow plunges.

The simple markings on the clock face are made by boring four holes into which small plugs are inserted to mark the hour, the quarters, and the half-hour. Plug making is done by using a plug cutter in the router, holding the work-piece securely before commencing the cut. Attach the Perspex sub-base (see page 79) before boring the clock face to receive the plugs, and take this opportunity to bore the centre hole to receive the boss of the clock unit.

Clean up carefully with abrasive paper and polish to suit. The router cuts should require little attention, but if papering is needed a small curved block should be cut to match them and the abrasive paper wrapped around them.

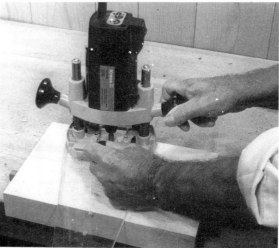

318 (above right) Using purpose-made Perspex trammel
319 (centre) Recessing the face with a core bit
320 (right) Face-cutting complete

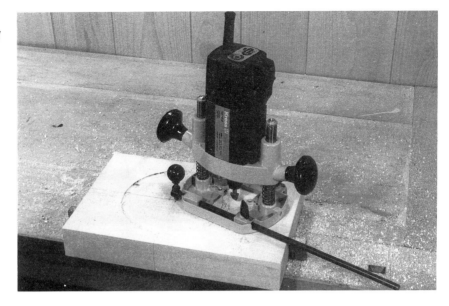

321 Elu 96 trammel bar could have been used instead

322 Template held in place with double-sided tape ready to guide the router in cutting the recess for the clock unit

323 Moving around the template

324 Recess cut to depth

Staircase

Whenever the business of making a staircase arises I become an obnoxious bore (some of my friends would say "So what's different?"). I believe I must be one of the very few people to have built a staircase for my mother's house in her garden, using timber bought with a licence, and a saw, a chisel, a mallet and a 'hammer-all' borrowed from a friend of the family. To crown it all: this was in the middle of the war and I was on seven days' leave. Yes, it's still there in all its Columbian pine glory as a monument to patience. When Sheila Kew asked me to make her one last year, I thought it might be a combined good test of improved conditions and the advent of the router.

We managed to find some splendid wych elm – yes, from a merchant in Devon, and the strings and stair treads were cut to size and accurately planed, coming out at 38mm (1½in) in thickness. Its location in the house was checked out, and the staircase angle of inclination arrived at.

I then made the staircase template which is shown on page 79; had I known than that Jim Phillips at Trend had the one shown on page 94 I would have borrowed it, since I'm basically a lazy man. The strings were marked so that the jig could be positioned, secured with G-cramps to the work bench, and my workshop cleared of all obstructions.

The jig had been cut with a specific size of router cutter in mind, and the bush guide selected to suit. These were attached to the router, and it was decided to make two passes to attain the depth of housing required. With eyeshield and mask in position the housings were completed in under two hours.

In designing the staircase, Sheila decided to use an ovolo shape to take away the sharp arrises, and, apart from the newel post which was just rounded over on its long corners, a 12.7mm (½in) cutter was used throughout. The handrail and other parts were treated similarly. Matching skirting, radiator hoods, and architraves were also made.

Finished in Danish teak oil, it looks a lot better than the standard parana pine job, and it cost a good deal less; but I'm not setting up as a staircase builder. The wife wants to move to a house so that she can have one, and it's just not on!

The angle of inclination, width of tread and headroom were all checked out with the Building Inspector before final plans were drawn.

326 Showing treads positioned in stopped housings

Decorative Window Grille

The method used in this project can be used in any number of different applications. I have used it elsewhere to produce table mats. A small window at the side of the house, overlooking the blank wall of the adjoining house, prompted this addition as a point of interest in an otherwise dull situation.

The design depends partly on the shape of the router cutter used, and on the number of passes the timber makes over it, together with the spacing of the passes and the depth of cut. The timber is worked on both sides; when the reverse side is being cut and the depth of cut has been arranged, the cutter breaks through into the cuts previously made, producing an attractive lattice work.

Choice of timber is important for this design; the grain should be fairly straight, free from knots and a wood which will not be affected too much by atmospheric conditions. A panel of mahogany, 22mm

327 *Decorative window grill*

(⅞in) thick, was cut and planed to make an exact fit against the existing wooden window frame. A strip of 16mm (⅝in) square mahogany was cut to make up the moulding to secure the panel in place. In order to prevent warping, a strip of beech was inserted in a groove cut along the end grain to a depth of 16mm (⅝in). Beech was chosen for its long straight grain and good strength.

The Elu router bench 551 was set up and the Elu 177 router secured in place. A 10mm (⅜in) panel router (straight) cutter was inserted in the collet, and the bench fence set at 6mm (¼in). Both panel ends were routed to make the grooves, great care being taken to hold the panel tightly against the fence and in an upright position. The strips were glued in place, and after the glue had set the ends were cleaned up.

The cutter was changed to a 8mm radius ovolo, and the depth gauge was set to 12mm (½in) for the first pass along the face of the panel with the grain, with the fence set to 25mm (1in). The panel was passed carefully across the cutter, making a cut from both edges. The panel was reversed, and with the fence remaining at 25mm, a cut was made across the grain; one at each end. The fence was re-set to 51mm (2in), and the procedure repeated on both faces of the panel.

Variations in settings are, of course, infinite and will depend on the size of the panel, the type of cutter, and the effect you wish to create. The ovolo cutter was replaced with a 6mm rounding-over cutter, and a small tunnel was made (see page 56) through which the moulding could be passed safely and held against the cutter. The tunnel was held against the fence using small cramps, and to ease the passage of the strip of moulding a touch of candlewax or paraffin wax was found helpful. The strip was cut to size carefully and the corners mitred carefully. Having cleaned up the panel, a suitable finish was chosen, bearing in mind the exposure to sunlight and also condensation. The panel was fixed with fine brass screws, which were countersunk screws, since the panel may have to be removed for cleaning or such like.

Many variations can be worked out, and if a small fixture is made to set against the fence, varying diagonal cuts can be taken.

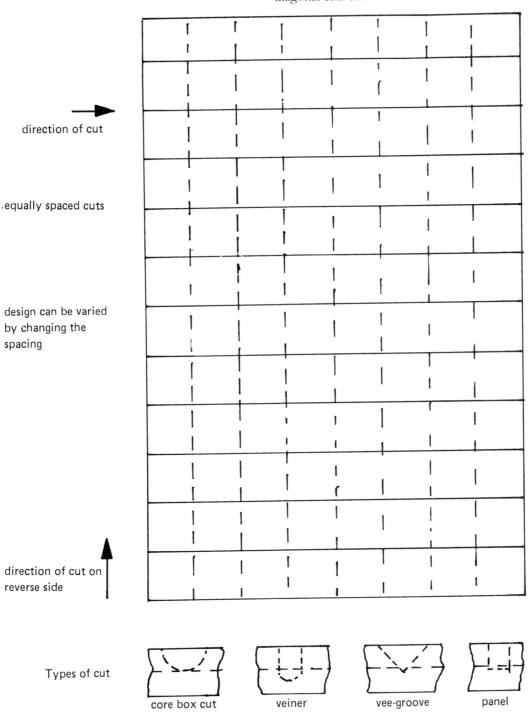

direction of cut

.equally spaced cuts

design can be varied by changing the spacing

direction of cut on reverse side

Types of cut

core box cut   veiner   vee-groove   panel

Teak Meat Board

A suitable timber must be chosen for this piece as some timbers could contaminate the meat or not be suitable for use in the kitchen. This one was made in teak and finished in a good quality cooking oil which preserves both food and board against contamination – it can be improved at any time by a further application of oil.

The board was first prepared by planing and sawing to exact size. Marking out consisted only of marking the points of start and stop for the router in pencil.

The router should be fitted with a cove cutter and the depth set for the outer gravy channel. With the straight fence fitted and set at the required distance of the cut from the edge, the plunge must be made and at the same time the periphery of the cutter sighted to strike in line with the start mark on the board. Ensure that the fence rides against the edge, and again carefully sight the cutter as it approaches the stop mark. Complete the cutting from all four sides. Remove the 15mm cutter and substitute a 10mm one, re-set the depth gauge to the depth required for the inner gravy channels, and fit the straight fence. Carefully cut each channel and watch the cutter carefully as it approaches the outer channels. When all cuts have been made remove the cutter and replace it with a straight two flute panel one. Remove the fence, set the depth to that needed for the gravy tray and rout out the waste. If the cutters are sharp very little cleaning up will be needed.

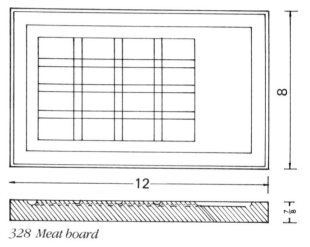

328 Meat board

329 Meat board

Occasional Table

Cutting list for occasional table (finished sizes)

	L	W	T		L	W	T
		mm				inches	
1 top	610	356	22		24	14	7/8
4 legs	381	25	25		15	1	1
4 rails	330	25	25		13	1	1
4 rails	559	25	25		22	1	1
2 slats	559	25	19		22	1	3/4

In teak or any suitable hardwood.

Designed in the traditional style, using the simple stopped mortise and tenon joint. Any attractive timber can be used but teak was available in this case. This job can be done using a number of proprietary jigs, but I am assuming here that the woodworker has only his basic router and has added to it one or two guides.

Prepare some square section timber of any size up to 32mm (1¼in) thick; this will be used for the legs and rails. A piece of timber 22mm (⅞in) thick is required for the top, rub-jointed or tongued and grooved to make up the required width if necessary.

The tenons are cut using a simple holding jig, details of which are shown in page 34. The rails are placed together in this jig and cramped up using folded wedges. Set up the router with a 12mm (½in) panel cutter; place the fence in position, measuring the distance from the edge of the jig to the shoulder line of the tenons. Set the depth gauge to a distance equal to one third the thickness of the rail material. Take a pass with the router across the full line of the tenons. Should the cut not be exactly the right width, depending on the actual length of the tenons, it will be necessary to re-set the fence and take a further cut. Remove the rails, turn them over, and cut the other cheeks. Set up the rails to cut the tenons at the opposite ends.

Another small jig can be quickly made to cut the mortises. A cutter which equals the actual width of the mortise must be selected, together with a suitable guide bush (the actual size must be chosen according to the width of the mortise). Three strips of softwood are used and slots cut as shown in Fig 242

330 Occasional table

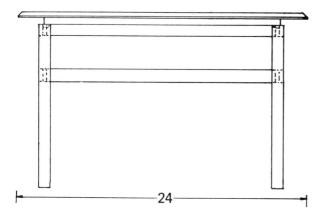

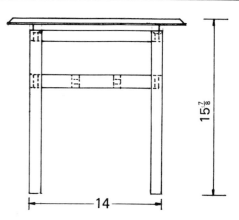

15⅞

24

14

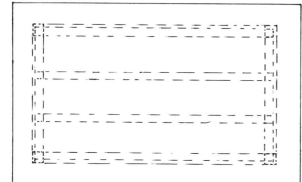

and the jig tacked together. It is made to fit exactly over each leg and is held in place with double-sided adhesive tape. This is an extremely accurate method of mortise cutting, and although the jig may not be used again it is so quickly made that the time factor can be ignored.

Mount an ovolo cutter of suitable size into the router, hold the table top securely, and rout the edges.

Clean up the work as necessary, glue up the frame and when the glue has set, add the top, securing it with a proprietary brand of bracket. On larger designs we would cut a number of blocks fitted with tongues, and insert them in grooves cut around the inside of the top rails, securing them to the top with screws.

Finally, choose a suitable polish to complete the job. Stand back and admire it and resolve to make another for the mother-in-law!

Occasional table and stool

Storage Chest

Bill of materials (finished sizes)

	L	W	T		L	W	T
		mm				inches	
A Front	914	305	19		36	12	3/4
B Back	914	305	19		36	12	3/4
C Sides	457	305	19		18	12	3/4
D Bottom (Cabinet grade plywood)	892	435	19		35 1/8	17 1/8	3/4
E Top edge strips on sides	419	32	19		16 1/2	1 1/4	3/4
F Lid	870	476	16		34 1/4	18 3/4	5/8
G Lid cleats (2)		51	19		16 3/8	2	3/4
H Base (2)	547	70	40		21 1/2	2 3/4	1 5/8
I Screws for attaching lid cleats (6) 6 x 1 in							
J Plugs for screw holes 6 – (12mm) 1/2 in dia.							
K Screws to secure bases (4) 8 x 3 in							
L Washers (4) 3/8 in dia.							
M Brass hinges (2)							
N Brass lid support							

Besides the obvious requirement of practising dovetail jointing, this start-up-project should be enjoyable to make and useful. The storage chest is universal enough that it will be 'at home' storing blankets, toys, memorabilia or tools. And because it is made with dovetails, it will have the beauty, durability and longevity to become a family heirloom.

There is no need to make hand-made furniture with inferior materials. The very essence of making things is that the maker has control over every aspect of the project. Selecting woods, adding or subtracting to the measurements, choosing hinges, or deciding upon staining or relief carving on the chest, are but a few choices open to the maker of hand-made furniture.

Storage chest

Selection of wood

Choose woods that exhibit a harmonious balance of colour, grain pattern, and surface texture. Other physical properties, such as timber straightness, flatness, and grain direction should also be considered.

The storage chest shown is made of red oak with teak as the accent wood. Select the primary and accent wood of your own preference. However, this is an exercise to familiarize yourself with the jig, so select woods which are not too expensive or difficult to work. Highly figured crotch or knotty woods, and woods of high density (hardness), such as hard maple, hickory or bubinga should be avoided for this project.

Notes on techniques

The joints used are: through dovetails, end-on-end dovetails (or keyed dovetails), grooves, and edge-to-edge gluing.

The widths of the chest sides and lid will require edge-to-edge gluing of separate boards. If the wood is perfectly flat, it may be possible to glue the pieces together and have no significant alignment problems. However, wet glue does allow wood to slide during the cramping process and there are a number of methods to keep boards in alignment, namely (a) full board length splines; (b) tongues and grooves; (c) plate or biscuit joints made with a biscuit jointer (more properly known as the hand jointer); and (d) dowels.

Choose the method with which you are familiar. For the lid, the additional design advantage of full length splines or loose tongues is that the spline can be made of a contrasting coloured wood, thus enhancing the edge's appearance. For the chest, select one of the other methods so that there will be no interference with the dovetails.

Notes on hardware

Select hinges and lid supports which best serve the use of the chest. If it is to be in constant use, select sturdy, well made hinges.

If it is for storing linens and blankets, select hinges and lid supports which will not snag on the material.

If it is to be a toy chest, there are a variety of lid supports available which control the descent of the lid, making it safe for children.

Brass hardware and screws are very attractive when used with the natural elegance of wood. Use Phillips or square-drive socket screws to avoid screwdriver slippage and unsightly damaged screw slots. Drill pilot holes for the screws, especially in hardwoods, to avoid splitting the wood.

331 Storage chest – joint detail

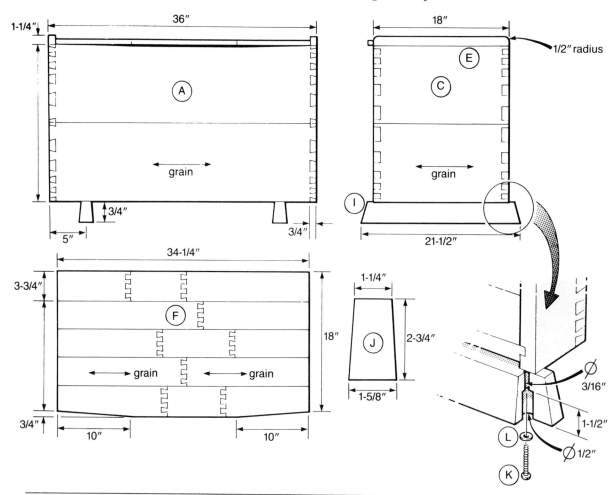

332 Hinge and lid support – detail

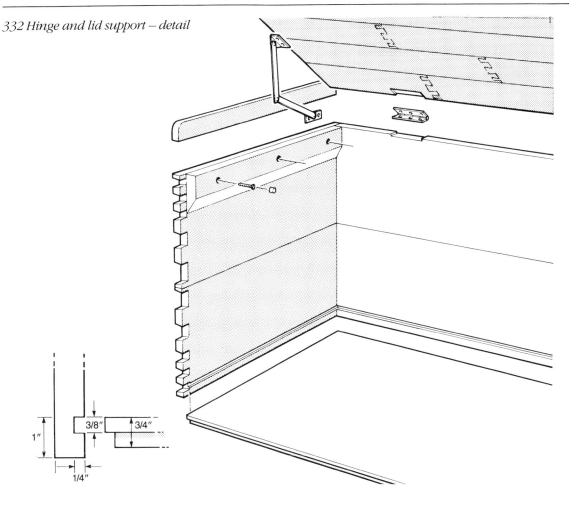

Use 'drywall' screws for attaching the lid cleats to the sides and attaching the two bases to the chest. These screws are made of hardened metal, have a needle point and sharp cutting threads. They also are meant to be driven with an electric screwdriver; the nearest equivalents in the UK are Supadriv screws.

Design options

The storage chest is attractive and functional as it appears in the plans. However, there are a number of optional designs which can be incorporated into it:

1 Changes in height, width, length;
2 Add sliding dovetail spacer walls (dovetail-housed sliding divisions) within the chest compartment;
3 Fit brass handles on either side;

4 Make a series of dovetailed stacking trays to nestle within the chest;
5 Line the chest with Incense Cedar;
6 Mix different woods in the lid's end-on-end dovetailed boards;
7 Add a lock.

Construction notes

To maintain straight and flat sides and also front and back panels, glue up two or three boards to equal the final width of 305mm (12in).

The best method for making the lid is to have five similar widths to equal the final width of 482mm (19in). Each of these widths should be made up of random short lengths. Before any end-on-end dovetails are cut, lay out all the random short lengths such that the overall lengths are about 1067mm

(42in). Make five different rows in a similar fashion. Move the various short lengths around until the arrangement has an attractive blend of colours and grain patterns. The chest lid illustrated has rows of 3, 2, 4, 2, 3 short lengths. The end-on-end dovetailed edges are randomly placed throughout the lid.

To attach the base units to the chest, drill over-sized screw holes through the bases and place washers on the screws. (The combination of over-sized holes and washers will allow the chest and bases to 'seasonally' expand and contract due to atmospheric changes perpendicularly to one another.) Make sure the screws are adequately tightened. Also, do not plug the screw holes after the screws have been attached. This will allow the base units to be removed for repairs or for moving, as necessary.

Dovetails

The chest carcase is constructed with through dovetails. Choose your own pattern of dovetails and cut them as described on page 162. With the Leigh Jig, the choice of dovetail sizes and spacing is infinite.

The lid is made up of random short lengths jointed together with end-on-end dovetails. Making end-on-end dovetails is actually the method of determining the depth of cut for half blind dovetails. However, for this project the benefits of the end-on-end dovetails are: the lid is made up of a series of short and narrow boards which will give tremendous stability (resists warping) to a 482mm by 876mm (19in by 34½in) lid. Finally, it will simply look great and will give the chest a balanced design theme – DOVETAILS!

333 Storage chest – joint detail

334 Storage chest

Glossary

Aloxite An abrasive used in the making of sharpening materials. Consists of artificial aluminium oxide which is obtained by treating the mineral bauxite in an electric furnace.

Baluster A small turned column which is part of a balustrade – the upright support for the handrail of a staircase.

Batten A piece of squared timber of small section usually about 50mm by 25mm (2in by 1in)

Bead A semi-circular moulding – usually of small section. Can be plain or decorated.

Bench stop A stop close to the end of the bench top against which the timber is held when planing. There are a number of different designs.

Bevel gauge A tool which can be set to produce any angle for marking out timber.

Bolection A raised and rebated moulding which projects beyond the face of the frame into which it is inserted.

Butt joint A joint made when two pieces of wood are joined together with no overlap, shoulders, or tenons.

Cabinet A piece of furniture which can be fitted with shelves or drawers or both. Many are fitted with decorative doors or glass panels. Usually associated with the display of choice articles of glass or china.

Capping A piece of timber, usually shaped and used to finish off the top of a post or rail.

Carcase The body part of a box-like piece of furniture minus the doors and fittings.

Cavetto A quarter-round concave moulding.

Chamfer A slanting or inclined surface produced by planing a square edge or corner equally on both sides. Chamfers may be through or stopped and are generally used as a decorative feature.

Collet A chuck using jaws to hold the circular shanks of cutters and bits.

Cramp or clamp (USA) Used to hold pieces of work together when gluing up. They can be in bar form or in the shape of the letter G. Mainly of metal construction with screwed components.

Cocked bead A bead (or astragal) which projects beyond the face of a panel; often fitted round drawer fronts.

Concave Hollowed out – the opposite of convex.

Contour The profile or section of a moulding.

Convex Having an exterior rounded shape – the opposite of concave.

Cornice The horizontal moulding which can be seen in the ceiling corners, or crowning the top of a cabinet.

Cove A concave moulding.

Dado (USA) Also called in the UK a housing – a wide grooved channel or trench cut across the grain.

Dowel Can refer to a headless pin of wood or steel, but used in woodwork, with an adhesive, to hold a joint together. Dowel joints – an alternative method of jointing.

Dowel bits Accurately-sized bits for cutting holes to receive dowels.

End grain The grain of the timber which shows when cut transversely.

Fence A guide used to regulate the movement of the router, keeping the cutter at an even distance from the edge of the work.

Fillet A small strip of wood used to support shelves, but also loosely applied to a narrow strip of timber fastened to the surface of a job to act as a fence when the router is working beyond the capacity of its own fence.

Fillister A kind of rebate used in sash window construction.

Frame The framework of doors or windows without the panels.

Gain (USA) The recess or housing used to accommodate a hinge or bracket.

G-cramp A cramp shaped like a letter 'G'.

Green wood Unseasoned timber.

Grinding Sharpening by holding an edge tool against a rotating wheel or belt.

Grounding Removing the background of a design which has to be carved – a job ideal for the router.

Handrail A rail as on a stairway used as a hand support.

Hardwood Deciduous trees generally give hardwood.

Heartwood The more durable wood (although this varies according to age and type) from the centre of the tree. The dead wood as opposed to the sapwood, which is the growing wood close to the bark of the tree and which carries the sap.

Heat treatment The heat treatment of metal refers to the processing through which steel goes from the time it is cast until it becomes a final product, and includes annealing, hardening and tempering. Heating changes the structure of the metal giving it important physical properties.

Annealing removes much of the internal stress induced by rolling or forging and brings the metal into a state where it will resist fracture. It results in maximum ductility and softness.

Hardening is the process of heating the metal to a certain temperature, then cooling it rapidly by quenching in water, oil, or some other medium to produce maximum hardness.

The degree of hardness in steel is often too great for many purposes and has to be modified, and this is brought about by re-heating to a known temperature. Tempering reduces hardness and brittleness and increases the ductility and toughness of the metal. Measurement of hardness can be gauged by a Brinell Test.

Hones and honing The hone (or oil-stone as it is more generally called) is made of a fine siliceous stone used for sharpening tool steel, and honing is using the stone for sharpening. Hones come in many shapes and sizes and in a variety of materials.

Hones for sharpening curved cutters come in various shapes and sections, while straight edged cutters are often sharpened by rubbing the stone on the cutter. The cutting action of the stone is due to the presence of quartz or silica; some stones are almost pure quartz, while in some stones the siliceous matter is mixed with aluminous or calcareous matter which gives an extremely fine edge on the tool. Minute particles of garnet or magnetite are sometimes present and these greatly assist the cutting action.

A hone of the finest quality, Arkansas, is found in Garland and Saline Counties, Arkansas, USA. The stones are about 98% silica with small proportions of alumina, potash, soda, and minute traces of magnesium, fluorine, lime and iron. Mainly whitish in colour, they are available as black hard, hard and soft grades, the black hard being suitable for the finest of instruments. Washita is a poorer grade of Arkansas which comes from the region of the Washita River, USA.

Housing Also called a channel – a wide trench cut across the grain to house a shelf or similar; called a 'dado' in the USA.

Knot A very hard mass in a piece of timber formed at the junction of a branch. Two kinds – the 'dead' knot which is loose and generally falls out, and the 'live' one which is firmly a part of the wood.

Matched boards or matching Boards which are cut with a groove running along one edge and a tongue running along the other. The joint is often broken by a bead cut along one edge of by both edges being chamfered to enhance the appearance. The router is ideal for making all these cuts.

Mitre The joining together of two pieces of wood at an evenly-divided angle usually but not necessarily 45°. A picture frame is a typical example.

Mouldings Stuck, these are worked on the job itself, while a planted one is added to the job either with glue or pins or both. See also *Bolection*.

Ogee This shape derives from architecture; it's a moulding having two curves which impart a wavelike profile formed by one convex and one concave curve.

Oilstone See *Hone*

Oilstone slip Used for sharpening curved cutters, and available in a variety of grits, including Rubberised.

Ovolo Another moulding, this one has a convex surface (as opposed to a cavetto) formed from a quarter of a circle or ellipse, with a listel.

Panel A board set in a frame – it can either be below, or above, or flush with, the face of the frame itself.

Parting bead A bead which is placed between the sliding sashes of a window. Also applied to a bead inserted between sliding doors to keep them apart.

Rail The horizontal member of a door or table carcase, or a chair frame.

Rebate (or rabbet in USA) An open-sided groove much used in frames which are panelled in glass.

Riser The vertical board at the front of each step or tread in a staircase.

Sapwood Living wood immediately under the bark of the tree which conducts the sap to the branches.

Sash A type of window frame.

Sash bars The strips which separate the glass in a sash window.

Shake A split in timber due to seasoning or stresses set up during felling, causing the wood to separate between the annular rings. The split running with the rings is called a 'cup shake'.

Slamming stile or strip The vertical strip of a door frame on which a door abuts when closed; it holds the lock-keep.

Softwood Wood from coniferous or needle-leaved trees.

Spalt Wood which is in decay through storage in wet conditions. It becomes short grained and breaks easily.

Staff bead A return bead worked on a salient angle, with a quirk at each side. Refers also to beaded strip which holds a sash window in place.

String One of the inclined members of a staircase into which the treads and risers are fitted.

Stub tenon A small tenon which does not go completely through the timber.

Tail vice A vice fitted at the end of a bench and generally used with dogs set both in the bench and in the vice itself to hold timber for planing and other jobs.

Temper see *Heat treatment*.

Tenon A projection at the end of a piece of wood which locates into a slot called a mortise in another piece thus holding them together when glued.

Torus A convex moulding of approximately semi-circular section, generally used as a moulding for the base of a cabinet.

Trench A channel or housing; called a 'dado' in the USA.

Tungsten This is a metal found in a number of minerals, but chiefly in wolframite. In colloidal form it is used in the filaments of lamps. As tungsten carbide it is used in a wide variety of cutting tools.

Vice clamps or pads An addition to the metalworking or woodworking vice to protect delicate work from being marked; they consist of small pads of wood, felt, or similar materials which can be attached temporarily or permanently.

Metric Conversion Table

INCHES – MM

Inches		MM	Inches		MM	Inches		MM
¼"	—	6 mm	7¼"	—	185 mm	40"	—	1015 mm
⅜"	—	10 mm	7½"	—	190 mm	41"	—	1040 mm
½"	—	12 mm	7¾"	—	195 mm	42"	—	1065 mm
⅝"	—	15 mm	8"	—	200 mm	43"	—	1090 mm
¾"	—	20 mm	8¼"	—	210 mm	44"	—	1120 mm
⅞"	—	22 mm	8½"	—	215 mm	45"	—	1145 mm
1"	—	25 mm	8¾"	—	220 mm	46"	—	1170 mm
1⅛"	—	30 mm	9"	—	230 mm	47"	—	1195 mm
1¼"	—	32 mm	9¼"	—	235 mm	48"	—	1220 mm
1⅜"	—	35 mm	9½"	—	240 mm	49"	—	1245 mm
1½"	—	38 mm	9¾"	—	250 mm	50"	—	1270 mm
1⅝"	—	40 mm	10"	—	255 mm	51"	—	1295 mm
1¾"	—	45 mm	10⅛"	—	257 mm	52"	—	1320 mm
2"	—	50 mm	11"	—	280 mm	53"	—	1345 mm
2⅛"-2¼"	—	55 mm	12"	—	305 mm	54"	—	1370 mm
2⅜"	—	60 mm	13"	—	330 mm	55"	—	1395 mm
2½"	—	63 mm	14"	—	355 mm	56"	—	1420 mm
2⅝"	—	65 mm	15"	—	380 mm	57"	—	1450 mm
2¾"	—	70 mm	16"	—	405 mm	58"	—	1475 mm
3"	—	75 mm	17"	—	430 mm	59"	—	1500 mm
3⅛"	—	80 mm	18"	—	460 mm	60"	—	1525 mm
3¼"	—	85 mm	19"	—	485 mm			
3½"	—	90 mm	20"	—	510 mm			
3⅔"	—	93 mm	21"	—	535 mm			
3¾"	—	95 mm	22"	—	560 mm			
4"	—	100 mm	23"	—	585 mm			
4⅛"	—	105 mm	24"	—	610 mm			
4¼"-4⅜"	—	110 mm	25"	—	635 mm			
4½"	—	115 mm	26"	—	660 mm			
4¾"	—	120 mm	27"	—	685 mm			
5"	—	125 mm	28"	—	710 mm			
5⅛"	—	130 mm	29"	—	735 mm			
5¼"	—	135 mm	30"	—	760 mm			
5½"	—	140 mm	31"	—	785 mm			
5¾"	—	145 mm	32"	—	815 mm			
6"	—	150 mm	33"	—	840 mm			
6⅛"	—	155 mm	34"	—	865 mm			
6¼"	—	160 mm	35"	—	890 mm			
6½"	—	165 mm	36"	—	915 mm			
6¾"	—	170 mm	37"	—	940 mm			
7" Fibre discs only	—	178 mm	38"	—	965 mm			
7"	—	180 mm	39"	—	990 mm			

To obtain the metric size for dimensions under 60", not shown in the above table, multiply the Imperial size in inches by 25·4 and round to the nearest millimetre taking **0·5 mm** upwards.

e.g. $9\tfrac{1}{8}" \times 25\cdot4 = 231\cdot8$
$= \textbf{232 mm}$

To obtain the metric size for dimensions over 60" multiply the Imperial size in inches by 25·4 and round to the nearest **10 mm** taking **5 mm** upwards.

e.g. $67" \times 25\cdot4 = 1701\cdot8$
$= \textbf{1700 mm}$

Router Speeds for Various Materials

The following table of electronic speed adjustments is merely a recommendation, since wood is a living material.

Even for the same types of wood there can be great differences in hardness and density.

★ best
XX very good
X good
O satisfactory
– not recommended

Material	Cutter dia.	Electronic Adjustments				
		Stage 1 8000 r.p.m.	Stage 2 12,000 r.p.m.	Stage 3 16,000 r.p.m.	Stage 4 18,000 r.p.m.	Stage 5 20,000 r.p.m.
Hardwoods, e.g. oak	small	–	–	O	X	★
	medium	–	–	O	X	★
	large	★	X	O	–	–
Softwood, e.g. pine	small	–	–	O	X	★
	medium	–	O	X	XX	★
	large	★	X	O	O	–
Plastic-coated chipboard	small	–	–	O	X	★
	medium	–	O	X	XX	★
	large	–	★	X	O	–
Plastic-coated panels	small	–	O	O	X	★
	medium	–	O	★	O	–
	large	O	X	★	O	–
Plastics	small	–	O	X	X	★
	medium	–	O	XX	★	X
	large	X	★	O	–	–
Aluminium	small	–	★	X	O	–
	medium	X	★	O	–	–
	large	★	X	O	–	–

Cup-shaped cutters					
Softwoods, e.g. pine	–	–	O	X	★
Veneered panels	O	X	★	O	–
Plastic-coated chipboard	X	★	O	–	–

Stages 1 to 5 refer specifically to the Elu Router 177E (see page 32).

For rapid feeds the electronic adjustment should be increased by one stage.

Bibliography

Router Handbook Patrick Spielman (Sterling, 1983)
Techniques of Routing Jim Phillips (International Thomson, 1986)
The Rockwell Router Rockwell Manufacturing Company (1968)

Video tapes
Router Jigs and Techniques Berni Maas and Michael Fortune, Fine Woodworking Magazine
Shopsmith Router Arm Shopsmith, USA only

Elu guide to routing Black & Decker Professional Division
Triton Mk3 Triton UK
Router Basics and Safety Bob Rosendahl, USA only
Table-mounting Your Router Bob Rosendahl, USA only
Router Jigs and Accessories Bob Rosendahl, USA only
Basic Routing by Roy Sutton
Advanced Routing by Roy Sutton
Fine Grain Productions Ltd

Acknowledgements

My especial thanks to Sheila Kew, my stand-in daughter for her painstaking reading of the proofs and keeping the English in line. To my wife for losing me for so many hours to the word processor. To David St John Thomas for persuading me to do it, to my Editor, Vivienne Wells, for suffering the consequences and to the staff at David and Charles for their patience. To Jim Phillips of Trend Machinery Ltd, Penfold Works, Watford for tremendous help with artwork and tools, particularly bearing in mind that he has a router book of his own to sell. To Linda Vian Smith at KWO Ltd, Sevenoaks, Kent for artwork. To John Costello and Neil Hamer of Black & Decker, Slough, Bucks, without whose help much of this book could not have been written. To Ken Grisley, an Englishman in Canada who supplied the Leigh Dovetail jig from Port Coquitlam in British Columbia, together with masses of help. To Allan Hughes Distributors of the Wallows Industrial Estate at Brierley Hill for the Keller Jig. To Steve Turner of A to Z Tools of Tamworth for some of the information about Sears tools when all at Sears were struck with silence. To Alan Young of Kress Power Tools. To M. K. Fisher at Micom of Malden in Essex for artwork. To both Richard Smidt and Connie Bland of the Porter Cable Corporation at Jackson in Tenessee who went out of their way to send help. Arthur Taverner of Hitachi Power Tools at Milton Keynes, Brian Neighbour of Robert Bosch Ltd, of Denham in Middlesex and Alan Lees of Makita Power Tools at Luton for artwork and equipment. Paul Merry of M & M Distributors of Haslam Crescent at Bexhill-on-Sea for rushing me a Triton workbench and answering my questions even on a Sunday. To Craft Supplies of Millersdale, Buxton. To Record Marples Tools at Sheffield. Gerry Baker of Luna Tools and Machinery at Bletchley, Milton Keynes also helped out with Ryobi. Geoff Brown of Brimarc Associates of Leamington Spa loaned Wolfcraft equipment and artwork. Paul Edelston was most helpful with artwork on the Dunlop Powerbase distributed from Felden Street in Glasgow. David Swallow of Clico in Shefield, Lervad Benches of Denham, Marten Baker of Spiralux in Gillingham, Kent helped with artwork and equipment. To Beth Saxon of Shopsmith at Dayton, Ohio for notes about the Router Arm. Stephen Skarsten at Skilten Tools of Welwyn in Hertfordshire for artwork. Roberta Larson of San Francisco. C. R. Onsrud. Attracta Products of the Hyde, London supplied the useful Multi-sharp sharpener. John Lovatt of Multistar Ltd, Stanway, Colchester with his woodturning chuck added adventure to routing on the lathe. P&J Dust Extraction of Revenge Road, Chatham solved the problem of removing the chips. Thanks also to John Gibson, Titman Tip Tools Ltd., Valley Road, Clacton-on-Sea for assistance in many ways and to Roy Sutton, Fine Grain Productions of Herne Bay, Kent for sight of the excellent videos on the Router.

I need to thank Bill Stankus living in New York for tremendous help with line drawings and photographs; he produced the instruction booklet on the Leigh Dovetail jig which is one of the best I have ever seen. Not forgetting Ann of Latent Image in Paignton Road, Liverpool for her care and patience in the laboratory processing my film.

Index

Page numbers in *italic* indicate illustrations